ON THE VERTIGO

One Sick Man's Journey to Make a Difference

A Memoir of
Sacrifice, Suffering, and Ultimate Triumph

Steven Schwier   David Schwier

ON THE VERTIGO

One Sick Man's Journey to Make a Difference

ISBN-13: 978-0-9913445-5-0

Published by

Blue House / Magoo

Dedicated to the memory of:

Raelynn Petrovich, Susan Davidson,
Larry Duncan and Christine King

You will not be forgotten!

ON THE VERTIGO

One Sick Man's Journey to Make a Difference

Prologue 1

PART 1 Colorado: Rocky Mountain High

Chapter 1...15
Chapter 2 22
Chapter 3 27
Chapter 4 28
Chapter 5 35

Flashback—2012..40

PART 2 Kansas: 1st overture

Chapter 6 42
Chapter 7 46
Chapter 8 51
Chapter 9 59

Flashback—2012..67

PART 3 Kansas: Second Overture

Chapter 10 69
Chapter 11 74
Chapter 12...79
Chapter 13...83

Flashback—2012 to 2013........................88

PART 4 Missouri: When it rains, it pours!

Chapter 14 90
Chapter 15...97
Chapter 16 109
Chapter 17...112
Chapter 18 116

ON THE VERTIGO

One Sick Man's Journey to Make a Difference

Chapter 19 121

Flashback—2014 129

PART 5 Illinois: God's country

Chapter 20 134
Chapter 21 140
Chapter 22 148
Chapter 23 156
Chapter 24 164
Chapter 25 170

Flashback—Summer 2015 174

PART 6 Indiana: The Hoosier State

Chapter 26 176
Chapter 27 180
Chapter 28 185
Chapter 29 190
Chapter 30 195
Chapter 31 201
Chapter 32 206
Chapter 33 216

Flashback—Summer 2019 224

PART 7 Ohio: Home State Homecoming

Chapter 34 226
Chapter 35 232
Chapter 36 237
Chapter 37 241

Epilogue 247

Ménière's

Gives:

Vertigo
Tinnitus
Hearing loss
Drop Attacks
Ear Fullness
Fatigue
Disequilibrium
Sensory Overload
and more...

Takes:

Your Energy
Your Friendships
Your Spontaneity
Your Social Life
Your Fearlessness
Your Quiet
Ability to Drive
Sense of Wellbeing
and more...

Meniere's Awareness Project

ON THE VERTIGO

One Sick Man's Journey to Make a Difference

PROLOGUE

2:15 a.m. September 5th, 2020

Day Five

Darkness wraps around me like putty. The moon is hidden and what stars I see are so faint they may as well not exist. I left the campsite five minutes ago and I'm already lost. I feel like I'm being squeezed by the night and have to remind myself to breathe . . . 1 . . . 2 . . . 3 . . . I'm somewhere in the middle of Kansas, but I might as well be on Mars. It's so black the headlamp that I wear and the headlight on my bike scarcely cut through the misty, dead air.

I feel alone.

The only company I have is the torturous, never ending jet engine blast in my left ear. It never goes away.

Ever.

Bugs are attracted to my light and sail in from every direction seeking excitement. I start to believe they too can hear the ringing in my head, as if the eternal metallic scream is being broadcast like a dinner bell inviting them to a grand feast. And that dinner is me. But, of course, they can't hear the ringing. No one can.

I pull to a stop because I remember my wife, Emily,

gave me a pair of safety glasses for such a time as this. When she handed them over I thought the gesture unnecessary. But now I send a silent thank you to the universe for her wisdom.

I unzip the small bag bungied on the back of my bike. It rides on a solid-frame carrier over the back fender. This arrangement looks like a third grader's Schwinn. But the bag is an invaluable part of my trip. It doesn't hold a lot, but it holds enough. I dig around for the clear lenses as I'm attacked on all fronts. Damn bugs! I slide the glasses on and start pedaling again. I'm instantly more relaxed.

Bobbing my head back and forth dodging bugs, I slam into swarms of space junk like I'm the Millennium Falcon preparing the jump to hyperspace. Gnats and mosquitoes collect in my hair, while the June bugs and moths bounce right off. Swallowing an occasional moth is no big deal; I need the protein. But the June bugs in Kansas are the size of gluttonous pigeons in Central Park, and not in short supply. I feel a little dizzy from the rioting insects, and that's not helping matters. It's time to get back to the business at hand, finding my way out of this dark and confusing campground.

I'm disoriented in my direction. And, if possible, I believe it's getting darker. There are no landmarks to help, and if there were I wouldn't see them anyway. It's day five of my twenty-five day trip, and I can't remember how to get out of this goddamn campground!

This could be a very long month . . .

Six months ago I came up with the idea to ride an E-bike from Denver, Colorado, to Columbus, Ohio: from where I live now, to where I grew up. The trip would cover 1,400 miles and take most of the month of September. I called my brother Dave two months ago and asked if he would quit his job to drive the support van. I explained I wanted to raise awareness and money for Ménière's Disease research. He's a year younger and has watched me live with this chronic illness for eight years. To my utter surprise, and complete terror, he said yes. I hadn't even told my wife at that point because if Dave said no, I'd scrap the whole thing. I'd go back to my couch. No problem. It's where I'd spent the last three years. Lying on my couch. Feeling like shit. And managing my symptoms. So this trip would probably sound like a fool's errand to Dave.

But, lo and behold, he said yes, starting an avalanche of logistical nightmares for me. The first problem was that I would need two batteries for my E-bike to make 100 miles a day. And that's only if the weather was good; with no wind, no hills and no vertigo attacks.

Oh, and by the way, each battery costs a cool one-grand. That's right, 1,000 green-backs . . . that I didn't have and had no idea how to get.

Yesterday at the end of my day's ride I took a left into Prairie Dog State Park, which is ten miles shy of Norton, Kansas. It was like a maze in a children's puzzle book trying to find our campsite. But tonight I'm doing it all in reverse.

In the pitch black a feeling of relief washes over me because I'm nearly to Route 36. Once there I'll take a right, point my bike due east, and I'm home free for the next 100 miles. A straight shot, my brain on idle.

For three days I've been on Route 36 straight out of Denver, and I'll be on it for another four hundred miles until the Missouri-Illinois border. Days away . . .

I turn right. I'm close to Route 36 and feeling confident. And that's exactly the moment I feel a thump in my gut. "Fuck, fuck, FUCK!" I say out loud. I forgot to pack my extra battery. I'll barely make it 30 miles.

I'm pissed and trying to stay under control.

Getting out of camp quietly without stirring my compadres was obviously too much to ask of myself. And now, I have to turn around and return to camp to retrieve my forgotten battery. This I do, lamenting every second of wasted time and energy. Forgetting to pack the extra battery was thoughtless. Now I'll have to re-navigate to the campsite in the dark.

I ride back the way I came, feeling like an idiot riding in circles, yelling at June bugs to leave me alone. For the love of God, I should not be out here by myself!

Ok, time out. Let's back up a couple hours . . .

It's midnight. I stare at the roof of my tent.

I've spent the last three nights in this tent since leaving Denver and it already feels like a permanent residence. It's a brown, mesh, two-person backpacking North Face tent. Did you get all that? Oh, and it has an orange rain cover. This will be my home away from home for the next twenty-five days minus six days in hotels to shit, shower and shave . . . minus the shave.

We're heading in to day five of my trip, and I took the whole day yesterday to rest. I crawled in my sack twenty minutes ago only to realize sleep would elude me.

I know this because I suffer from insomnia. I turn into a monster. I become Dracula. A werewolf. The Loch Ness Monster. I become a boogeyman that scares kids in the night when things don't feel right.

And I don't feel right! Ever!

I get insomnia all the time. It doesn't sound like such a bad thing. But insomnia is something that is mentally debilitating for someone with Ménière's. Being

4

awake for 48 hours does something to a person's psyche. Something happens in the human soul between the hours of 2 and 5 a.m. and it's never good. These are the witching hours when my mind races and I can't stop it. I doubt myself and who I am. My very existence becomes surreal. I haunt myself into insanity.

It was like that tonight.

I stare at the cargo hammock hanging inside my tent. It holds my Chapstick, my winter cap, my cell phone, and the grey oval container where my hearing aid sleeps. I only wear one in my left ear, because the left is the only one permanently damaged. Everything has to be in its proper space because I get stressed easily. So setting up my tent is a lesson in Obsessive Compulsive Disorder. (It's actually not OCD, but it probably looks like it.)

Waking up in the middle of the night, nauseated, dizzy, and with a ringing ear, I don't have the energy to dig around in my tent to find what I need. Managing my stress is a full-time job. It's part of who I am. At the end of the day I can't rest until my tent is set up exactly how I need it.

Anxiety plays a huge part in how I manage my day as well. Anything I can do to alleviate anxiety is what I put all my energy into. Insomnia wreaks havoc with my anxiety, and distraction is the answer. It's a constant juggling act. Deciding to ride a bike from Denver to Columbus, I knew I had created one big circus.

Tonight, riding my bike would become my distraction.

At home the distraction would be late night info-mercials. Companies peddling anything from shitty vacuum cleaners to super glue that will patch a hole in your yacht or keep your ass from sagging. I came up with the idea for an E-bike ride six months ago, but now reality is hitting hard. Now we're in the trenches, and I'm starting to feel the pressure.

We rented a van as a support vehicle, and so Dave would have a roaming office. Oh, and did I mention it'd be his bedroom as well? Yeah, he rigged a bunk, and it looks quite comfortable. My friend of 20 years Bill also decided to join us for the first week of the trip. I unfairly delegated these guys with the job of keeping me healthy and sane, while I attempted to ride my E-bike 1,400 miles.

The first three days went very well for the most part. I made it 100 miles each day. We were finding our rhythm. But tonight was different. Tomorrow I was staring down a 100 degree day and insomnia had taken its hold. I can only stare at the inside of my tent for so long, so after a couple hours of this I decided I'd ride. The three of us had decided before we hit the sack that I'd leave at 5:30 a.m. to beat the heat. Now I'd really beat the heat! I would start my hundred miles at 2 a.m. by myself, and this was going to throw a massive wrench into the monkey.

For one, I would be responsible for my own battery change. This meant I needed to carry it on my person. I'm throwing a curveball here. Dave went to bed at 9 p.m. after watching my sorry ass ride 300 miles in three days and taking care of everything I needed. He spends hours updating our social media. He needs his rest.

Bill on the other hand, has volunteered to be our scout. He rides his Harley Davidson 2010 Deluxe, and carries all his camping gear with him. We stay up almost till midnight each night, drinking beer and chatting about the day and life in general. He drives 100 or so miles ahead unless I have an emergency. He finds a place to camp so Dave and I can focus on my bike and keeping

6

me alive. That's how we ended up at Prairie Dog State Park in Norton, Kansas, on our third night.

My concern now at 2 a.m. is getting on my bike and riding without waking up the guys. I pack my tent and start to gather my belongings. I don't think my leaving at this time would go over well with either of them. I put a lot of pressure on them to keep me healthy, safe, and on my route. Me deciding to take off at 2 a.m. probably wouldn't sound like the brightest idea. We're talking about riding 90 miles solo, most of it in the dark with no support team.

That is not advisable under any normal circumstances.

And I don't live under normal circumstances.

Ménière's Disease (MD) has the upper hand on this trip. If you won't let me sleep then I'm not going to lie awake in my tent all night thinking about you. I'm going to ride my bike and distract myself. So fuck you, MD!

I spend the next 15 minutes getting my shit together trying to be as quiet as possible. Packing each day for my ride is usually pretty elementary, but doing it in the dark with only my headlamp is quite a challenge.

All I really need is my ass-pack. It's a butt pack on steroids. It holds two empty Gatorade bottles that I fill with water, a pouch of beef jerky, a banana, two peanut butter sandwiches and various other odds and ends. I also need my phone, and a portable charger which we call 'the brick.' I also wear headphones to protect my ears from the wind and road noise. The headphones connect wirelessly to my cell phone so I can listen to music and take calls. They also have a dropdown mic so I can talk to the support team, or my family, as I ride.

So I'm gathering things up like a squirrel with a stick up its butt when suddenly the back door of the van opens and Dave pops out. I think 'Oh, shit!' and brace for

7

an argument, a disagreement, or just flat-out 'What the hell are you doing?'

But instead, Dave says, "What's happening?"

I say, "I can't sleep. I've got insomnia. I just want to start riding."

Instead of battling me on this, Dave says, "What can I do to help you get going?"

This was the point I knew the trip could be a success. Because at that point Dave trusted me. He trusted me to do what I needed when I needed to do it. It gave me that same feeling when your dad says, 'Hey, Sport, I'm proud of you.' And that's priceless. Dave helps me finish packing and sends me on my way.

Before I leave he says, "I have my phone close, call if you need anything. I'll be right there." And with that, he crawls back into his van cave and goes back to sleep.

Now I'm at the park entrance realizing I forgot the extra battery so I'll have to return to camp.

Fuck!

It was a shitshow finding my way out of the campground the first time—taking me forever to find the exit and now I realize I hadn't grabbed the extra battery. This is a problem.

The battery for my E-bike lasts between 30 and 50 miles depending on weather and/or exertion. So every 40 miles or so Dave has to meet me with the van to switch batteries and start charging the dead one. Leaving at 2 a.m. with only one battery I'd be out of power and dead in the water by sunup.

Forgetting the spare battery back at camp was a huge brain fart. Standing at the park exit, I had a decision to make: Go on without the battery, or go all the way back to camp and get it. I didn't want to have to wake Dave at 6 a.m. and have him drive an hour to switch the battery.

I was hoping he and Bill could sleep in, pack up camp, take it easy, and meet me around the 90 mile mark.

Dammit. Now I'm going back for the extra battery.

I'm angry. I head back to our campsite, which I had a hard time finding in the light much less in the dark. I've been on my bike less than 20 minutes and I'm disgusted at the time wasted. I start making turns left and right, and once again I'm a mouse looking for the cheese. Battling my situation—thick with bugs, my physical limitations, the never-ending ringing in my ears, the balance issues—I'm already nauseous and disoriented and I haven't even started my day yet.

I finally make it back to our campsite and it occurs to me the extra battery I need is in between the front seats of the van.

Well, shit.

I woke Dave once already and I know as soon as I open the door the interior light will wake him again for sure. This just makes me feel worse, but I have to do it if I'm going to have power to ride all night.

As gingerly as possible, I open the passenger door. The overhead light blazes like the sun. Dave lifts his head, "Is everything OK?"

Like an ass I say, "Sorry to wake you again, but I forgot the battery. I've only been gone 20 minutes. Go back to sleep and call me when you wake up."

I slide the battery into my backpack (which is really a pouch with strings) and somehow navigate the labyrinth once again.

Left turn, right turn, left turn. 'Just keep going uphill,' I tell myself.

Next thing I know, for the second time tonight I'm at the park exit to State Route 36. I haven't worn a backpack during my first 300 miles, and it's awkward to say the least. The ten-pound battery in my string bag digs into my back and I keep fidgeting and readjusting. Knowing I'm back on Route 36 helps me relax, and the feeling of freedom settles over me. I turn right and start the ten mile ride towards Norton.

It's 3 a.m. and heading east once again feels good. I fall into my rhythm. I'm pedaling. At this point I don't have to think too hard, I just need to stay straight and not die.

I quickly realize I love riding at night and in my head I've already left my campground shenanigans far behind. I feel safe with my headlight and headlamp. I also have two rear lights that will alert the one car that will pass me in the next three hours. I've got my headphones playing smooth jazz to keep me calm and focused.

For the first time tonight I think today is going to be a good day.

Dave:

Early in the spring of 2020 Steve called me and said he wanted to do a fundraising/awareness bike trip across America—from, say, Los Angeles to the East Coast. Somewhere like North Carolina or something. It'd take a couple months or so, and we'd do it around this time next year so we had plenty of time to plan.

"Wow," I said.

That's pretty wild, I thought. But we'd have a year to think about it.

"I'm still just thinking about it," Steve said then. "So don't tell anyone."

"Ok," I agreed.

Then in June I got another call from Steve. He was in Denver, I was in Columbus, Ohio.

"I want to do the trip in September. It'll be from

Denver to Columbus and we'll do it in a month. Oh, and I'm going to ride an E-bike."

That's two months away, I thought. Hmmmmmm.

We discussed it some more and I ended with, "Ok, let me think about it and I'll call you in the next couple days."

"Oh, and I still haven't told anyone."

"Ok."

We ended the call and I walked back up my nephew Nathan's driveway to the porch where he and my younger brother Brian were hanging out.

"Ok," I said, feeling like I was about to ask them if they thought it was possible to slingshot myself to the moon and back using a rubber band and some duct tape. "Steve says he wants to ride an E-bike from Denver to Columbus, and do it in a month."

"When?" my nephew asked.

"September. This September."

They both leaned back.

"And he wants me to go."

"What's an E-bike?" my brother asked.

"I don't know. It's an electric bike, I guess. Probably like a moped."

They stared into space again.

"What I need from each of you is your opinion of whether you think he can make it." I looked at my nephew, "Go."

"Ahhh, well," he began tentatively. "I guess what really matters is if HE thinks he can make it. If he thinks he can make it, then sure. Why not."

I looked at my younger brother, "You?" Personally, I was fighting major doubts and waiting for one of them to say, 'Yeah, there's no way.'

I've been with Steve off and on (more on than off) since he was diagnosed eight years ago. Not only that, but my younger brother was with us at a New Year's get-

11

together at a friends house in Colorado last year when Steve had a major vertigo episode on the couch. Brian and I carried him out of the house to the car. At that time the guy weighed about a buck-0-five, and when we positioned ourselves under both arms, it was like lifting a shirt.

Before he could respond, I said, "My concern is that he weighs next to nothing because he doesn't eat. How is he going to generate the calories each day to pull this off?"

Steve doesn't eat because no one wants to eat when they're carsick, and he's carsick all of the time.

And I mean: All. Of. The. Time.

"Hmmm," my brother leaned back in thought.

"And what if a vertigo attack hits when he's in traffic?" I hadn't even let my brother speak yet, but continued anyway, "But if he doesn't have to pedal," I reasoned, "and just has to make sure he stays upright and doesn't go under a truck, then he should be all right." But I still wasn't convinced.

My brother looked at me, "But it's like Nathan said, what matters most is if he thinks he can make it."

"But can we really put a trip like that together in two months? Is that even possible?" I thought we'd have a year. And even that was pushing it. They both shrug and stare again. We ended it at that and went on to other things.

I called my father later that night and he was pretty confident right off the bat. "I think he can do it." I was taken aback by his unflinching confidence, but I've also been with Steve more than anyone else since he's been sick.

But with three votes of confidence in my pocket, I called Steve and told him I'd do it.

So we started planning.

But my initial agreement was based on the assumption that an E-bike was pretty much a moped—that it would power itself, so he'd just have to keep himself upright. If I'd have known it was pedal-assist, meaning you had to pedal the whole time or it wouldn't go at all (something I didn't find out till I got to Colorado), honestly, I think I might've said no.

But maybe not.

Because ultimately, to me, this wasn't about whether Steve could make it or not, but about the fact that I'd seen him suffer this horrible condition for so many years and it didn't really matter what he wanted to do, I'd help him succeed no matter how far-out or crazy it seemed.

PART 1

Colorado: Rocky Mountain High

Denver Tech Center to Anton, Colorado, 103 miles

CHAPTER 1

8 a.m., September 1st, 2020

Day One

I don't feel normal around people. I don't hear what they hear. I don't see what they see. And I sure as hell don't feel what they feel. I have a new normal and it's nothing like the old normal. Deciding to do this trip was a way of giving Ménière's a big, fat middle finger. I'm giving myself one month to create my own normal and we're going to play by my rules now. I'm putting myself in every situation that I fear. I'm telling my chronic illness You Don't Own Me, not this month you don't. You're on my court now, Ménière's, and there are no rules.

My only rule is that I'm going to do this my way. Anyway I want. All you naysayers and advice givers be damned. This isn't about you. This is one V one, mono y mono, me against my disease.

The problem is I'm giving the disease a head start.

I'll be putting myself in every situation I hate to be in—weather changes, extreme heat and cold, unpredictable barometric changes, loud noises, high winds, speeding trucks, constant motion, physical exertion, fighting balance issues, staring at a white line

for hours on end till it starts playing tricks on my eyes.
   But I hate to lose.

   Meeting John, a fellow Ménière's sufferer, this
morning at my sister's place in Denver where we started
was an out-of-body experience. I was diagnosed eight
years ago and I've never met another person with
Ménière's face-to-face. He became aware of my trip
after discovering it on social media. We didn't
communicate much before meeting. After exchanging a
couple of emails, he said he'd like to start my ride with
me. I told him, 'Okay, we leave September 1st around
10 a.m., give or take,' and I gave him the address. I
thought the perfect place to start my trip would be
Pantera Plaza, where my sister lives, a high-rise
apartment building in the Denver Tech Center.
   The plan was, Dave and I along with Bill would
spend Monday packing the support van up in Summit
County where I live. This included a featherlight racing
bike Dave borrowed from his friend Bryce, my E-bike,
our packs with of our clothes and personal belongings, a
cooler for food and beverages, and Dave's hastily built
bunk with a mattress raised high enough to allow storage
underneath. (This one move saved us so many
headaches, I can't even tell you . . .) We also had a clear
plastic tub filled helter-skelter with extra parts. This
included four new tires, four inner tubes, a box of chain
lube, extra hand grips, mirrors, and an assortment of
other things I thought I might need.
   Being the amateurs that we were, and having only
given ourselves one month to iron out the details of a
cross-country bike ride, we really had no idea if we were
over-packed or under-packed, headed for travel bliss or
heading down shit's creek and off a waterfall. But to hell
with it, we were excited to finally get going.

Everything packed, Monday evening we headed down from Summit County to Denver. I lived an hour West of Denver and four thousand feet higher in elevation. I thought it wise to start on as flat of ground as possible, probably more out of fear and anxiety than anything else.

My wife, myself, and my 18-year-old son Nolan drove our Xterra to a hotel across the street from my sister's. Dave drove the support van and met us at the hotel. In retrospect, this worked out very well. We could all get a good night's sleep, get up, cross the street to my sister's, and have a quick send-off breakfast.

Bill rode his Harley down and stayed at his aunt's house, near my sister's condo. Bill volunteered to be part of the support team to ride ahead as an all purpose scout, snack finder, camp spot finder, and amateur bike mechanic. Him deciding to join us was huge. We were lucky to have him. He committed to one week, but lucky for us it stretched into two.

My sister lived on the 24th floor of their high-rise. For someone with Ménière's, the last thing you want to do is step onto an elevator.

At 8:30 a.m. the morning of September 1st, I went up, said "Hi" to my sister, then took the horror box back down to meet Bill in the parking lot. I saw Bill, but noticed another vehicle as well. I told Bill to stand by and started walking across the lot. I thought I knew who this was.

"Are you John?" I asked.

He said "Yes," and we embraced.

John was diagnosed with MD more than 30 years ago. He's also bilateral, which means he's affected with this torturous illness in both ears. This was the very first time either of us had met another person in real life with Ménière's.

17

It was a bit overwhelming.

My brain exploded with a million questions. But now was not the time or place. I felt an instant kinship with him. He was 52 and a year younger than me. He and his wife were raising a beautiful fifteen-year-old daughter. He was fit and athletic. He was dressed head to toe in real biking apparel. I could tell he could put some serious miles on a bike. Maybe I should send him to Columbus and I could get back to my couch. Just a thought. Him showing up as a show of support was amazing.

John, myself and Bill walked back inside, I fobbed the elevator again, and we rose up slow as molasses. I glanced at John to see if he was as uncomfortable as I was in an elevator. He seemed OK, so I kept my mouth shut.

My sister, Karen, her husband, Garth, my wife, Emily, my son, Nolan, our good friends Bryce and Isabel, and of course Dave, Bill and John who we met in the parking lot, were chit-chatting and munching on bacon. This would be everyone riding with me for the start of my journey. Oh, and my niece Jennica was there who would head to work after breakfast.

Knowing he used to be a competitive bicycle racer, Dave invited his friend Bryce along for the first day. We figured maybe he'd just ride out of town and back, but he was excited. Super excited. Maybe he'd go for longer? Turns out we'd have him for four days.

I looked around the room. Everyone there knew about my battle with Ménière's Disease, but they'd only ever heard it from me. This felt like a defining moment.

Had I been deceiving myself all these years?

Was I just making this shit up?

Was my suffering for real?

My anxiety kicked up a notch and I wondered: What if John said, 'I've had this disease for 30 years and it's just not that big a deal?' But when I looked him straight in the eyes, I could see it. It was right there on the surface, plain as day. This man suffers, and suffers greatly.

Dave asked John for permission to film our interaction and John graciously agreed. We fired questions at him and he answered with unembarrassed honesty. I began to feel vindicated.

That's the only word to describe it: vindication.

Not in the snotty prideful way, but just the opposite; a humbling vindication. As in, I'm not alone. And it fires me up even more to see this trip through.

As John described his battle with this illness I felt as though I was looking in a mirror. We both teared up at times, but mostly me. It was like we were aliens from outer-space separated at birth and finally finding each other again.

Here.

Now.

And it was wonderful. He tilted his head at odd angles so he could understand the questions we fired his way and I was sympathetic to the energy he was expending.

With some food in our bellies, our whole crew headed down to saddle up and ride. I looked around. A pretty big group.

The days leading up to this had been a little stressful. I suffer severe anxiety, and because of Ménière's my self-esteem isn't the sharpest. Having this group of people riding with me today was sort of a paradox. There was a kind of party atmosphere, but I was also staring down 1,400 miles. This was on my mind more than anything. Can I do this? Can I even make it 100 miles today? If I can't make it a hundred miles today, then what's the use?

As everyone pulled bikes from cars, checked their tires and strapped on gear, I was kind of a hot mess. I wanted to spend time with every single person, to let them know how much I appreciated their support.

But a part of me wanted to be free.

I just wanted to start riding and get this shit show on the road. Does that seem selfish? I think it does. But the job ahead seemed insurmountable and I was shitting bricks. A good friend said, 'Just enjoy it. These people care about you and your trip. Take it slow and easy and enjoy it.' I carried those words for 1,400 miles.

My sister, her husband, and I were on electric bikes. The others were on an assortment of regular bikes, mountain bikes, and ten-speed racers. Dave had a GoPro strapped to his head filming the entire event.

I was amazed and impressed that John chose to ride the first 20 miles on his ten-speed before turning around. It was a pleasure to have him involved. We had an eclectic start to what would become, I was hoping, one of the greatest adventures of my life.

We left the parking lot looking like a Denver chapter of Hells Angels, minus the leather, tattoos, motorcycles, and any power of intimidation. Bill was the only one that fit that stereotype, being six foot one with a solid build. His head was shaved bald and he wore the whole biker outfit. And he actually *was* riding a Harley.

As the miles went on, people faded away or turned back because they had a job or a life to live. For the next month this was the life I chose to live.

And I wasn't ready.

I was, however, looking forward to seeing what was going to happen. The people I'd run into, the lives I'd impact and those that would impact me.

At the end of my first 23 miles it was just me and my brother-in-law slowly creeping east toward Kansas.

Only 1,387 more miles to go!

Soon he and I were by the side of the road hugging it out. He had to return to the real world as I continued to pedal toward God knows what.

Bill sped past on his Harley to find us a place to camp for the night. A pang of jealousy hit me, yet it did my heart good to see him twist the throttle with authority and shoot down the road in a cloud of dust.

I've known Bill for 20 years. We've raised our kids together and been on numerous motorcycling adventures. 'Man, I love that guy,' I thought to myself.

Dave had turned back miles ago to get the support van and bring it forward. For the first time since coming up with this crazy idea, I was alone.

All alone.

Just me, my bike, the road, and the music in my headphones . . . I can't help but pedal and smile!

CHAPTER 2

I'm 53-years-old and fairly athletic, but I've never ridden a bike 100 miles.

Ever.

I'm not now, nor have I ever been, an avid cyclist. I don't have a cyclist physique. In a past life, I weighed 175 lbs, which worked well for my five-foot-ten-inch frame. Now I weigh in at just over 150 and have lost nearly all of my muscle mass.

My wife and I have mountain bikes. We ride a handful of times each summer, but nothing like this. My mountain bike is a bright green Gary Fisher model that's 20 years old. After five to ten miles I'd be exhausted from the sheer exertion. Add to that the energy and focus needed for my balance, and 100 miles is impossible.

Maybe in my past life.

Discovering the E-bike, however, opened up all kinds of possibilities, and I fell in love. As long as I peddle, the electric assist helps me along. It's not a motor, it's an assist. If I don't pedal, I don't get help. Taking the energy of physical exertion out of the equation allows me to cover more ground. I can focus more on my balance. This takes a lot of concentration. I found a freedom in the E-bike I haven't had since my days riding motorcycles. And those days are long gone, a love that was taken away too early.

But 100 miles is 100 miles no matter how you package it. If I can't do 100 miles a day, this trip would take months. And that is out of the question. I have a wife and son. I have travel expenses. This trip needs to happen within a month or no dice.

My wife, Emily, and I spent a whole evening the weekend before the trip plotting my route. We sat on our couch with a map and my phone. Anton, Colorado, is exactly 100 miles from my sister's front door, and this town became my initial obsession. We subsequently plotted towns 100 miles apart for the rest of my trip.

In addition to questions of endurance, Ménière's has also robbed me of my agility. Some days I need the assistance of a cane. Other days, I hold on to walls, kitchen counters, and furniture as I pass by. I lost all cognitive balance in my left ear years ago. My right ear has since bore the responsibility of keeping my entire body upright.

My reality is hard to explain: Picture a drunken sailor stumbling out of a seaside pub after a night of tying one on, stumbling back to his ship, wobbly and unsteady as he traverses the boardwalk as best he can. That's me on a good day. But since I'm not a pirate, or a drunken sailor, you can imagine the looks I often get in public. But if you need to stare, or mumble under your breath in my direction, go ahead! I'm just trying to get through my day without breaking a hip. Which is a very real possibility if I stop concentrating.

The competitive sports I used to participate in are a thing of the past, a different life. I was robbed of it long ago. If I can sit up straight and get out of bed in the morning, I deserve a trophy-I can see it in my mind: it's a broken, crooked piece of wood with a silver plastic man on top using a cane. Ahh, sweet victory.

Deciding to ride a bike, even an E-bike, 100 miles a day for a month is ludicrous. Doubt sets in hourly as the Monster reminds me I'm not my old self. It whispers in my ear—yeah, that one, the one that rings so loud I feel like I'm standing next to Tom Cruise's F-14 Tomcat in *Top Gun*—it says: *You're broken. You're weak. You don't have what it takes. Go back to your couch, you pussy, because that's where you belong!*

That's when I look straight into MD's dizzy,

nauseous, vertigo-loving eyes and say Fuck You! Not this month. You might kill me, but if you do, I'm taking you down with me! This is what I signed up for, so let's dance, Fucker!

CHAPTER 3

For a month I've pictured myself alone and conquering the entire Midwest by myself.

A lone wolf, a renegade. Me, myself, the wind, and sheer will power.

Not hitting the 100-mile mark on the first day would push me over the edge. In retrospect it was a good thing I had a group of friends and family set the pace at the beginning or I would've come out of the gate with my ass on fire and burned out after 40 miles. The weight of not making the 100 miles on the first day would've overwhelmed me.

Yes, I'm that competitive.

So we started from Denver with nine bikes at a nice, easy pace. This proved invaluable to my first 23 miles. It kept me distracted and relaxed. I rode up and down the line of bikes casually talking with friends and family one at a time, not once thinking of the 100 miles ahead. We glided through the city on bike paths and calm streets, like a snake slithering to its destination.

At one point John and I chatted some more about our disease and how it's stripped us of so much. Before peeling off, my son Nolan said he was proud of me and it felt great. My wife and I said we loved each other, and then she turned back. It was a bittersweet moment in my ride so far.

When you suffer a chronic illness, support from family and friends is everything. They know my suffering, they know my fight, and their support is paramount. I felt relaxed and comfortable and before I knew it, 23 miles were behind me as I glided into Watkins, Colorado.

CHAPTER 4

I'd be on Route 36 from Watkins, Colorado, all the way to Illinois. It crosses my mind that Dave should be grabbing the van back in Denver about now and catching up soon. Bryce would be grabbing his truck and heading for Anton. He wants to ride alongside me on one of his race bikes for the next several days while leap-frogging with his truck. I haven't seen Bill or his Harley since he waved us on from a small park in east Denver, but he should be well on his way to Anton as well to secure us a campsite for tonight.

Since we took it easy for the first 23 miles, I have enough battery to get me to the 50 mile mark. This is good, and I'm looking forward to seeing if all will go as planned. I've imagined every nightmare scenario that could go wrong:

Will my bike go 100 miles without breaking down?

Will the first battery switch go off without a hitch?

Will we be able to get a campsite for tonight? There's only one campground within 100 miles of Anton, if we can't stay there, then what?

And lastly, will I be able to concentrate for eight hours and not die. My anxiety mounts thinking of all this, so I tell myself, "One thing at a time, Dipshit."

But those fears aside, I've enjoyed my last three hours; the weather is good and I'm feeling confident. There are a lot of firsts for this trip and most are going to happen today.

I pull my phone from my shorts pocket and dial Dave.

This is another first: Can I contact the team and can they contact me?

I pull down the microphone attached to my headset and to my surprise Dave answers. He sounds clear and I don't lose a beat. Other than not getting hit by a truck or dying, this is the first hurdle I jumped and it feels great.

"Where are you?" I ask.

"I just went through Watkins," Dave replies. "Where are you?"

"You'll pass me in 30 to 45 minutes. And I'll be ready for the switch."

"Okay I'll watch for you and stop at the next safe place. How's it going so far?" he asks with concern.

"Doing well. I'll keep an eye out for you," I reply.

I ride on, glancing in my side mirror. Traffic is light and I have a wide, clean shoulder to ride on.

I hope it's like this all the way to Columbus!

I hang up my phone, crank up my music and keep my rhythm. I arrive in the town of Strasburg before Dave catches me. I park my bike next to the post office. There is a two-foot high brick ledge in the shade. It also faces the street. A perfect place to rest and wait.

I call Dave and give him my location. He's 20 miles out and should arrive in the next fifteen minutes or so. In the meantime, I eat some jerky and enjoy sitting still. Dave easily spots me and pulls the van into a parking space directly in front of me. This is the first time we swap batteries and it has to work, a moment of truth.

The key that unlocks my battery is hooked to the rental van key chain. We sure as hell don't want to misplace that. Dave hands me the key like he's done this a million times.

Me, not so much.

My hands are shaking. When you have MD, it's hard not to expect the worst. This is the first chance the Monster has to throw a punch and I'm on high alert.

I nervously grab the key. Dave reaches between the seats and gets the fully charged battery that sits on the floor. We have a 110 outlet in the dash and will start charging the drained battery as soon as we're done.

I put the key in the slot on the frame that's just above the battery on the left side of my bike. I turn it slowly with shaky fingers. I feel a slight pop and pull the battery upwards at an angle hoping it slides loose. My heart is pounding and I'm afraid to rush and damage a connector. I gingerly slide the battery up and out like I'm picking up a sleeping baby.

Step 1, check.

We named the batteries Blackie and Pinky; one is black, one is Pink, so go figure. I cradle Pinky, who is drained down to 7%, and pass it off like it's a live bomb.

'Be careful, be careful, be careful,' I think. 'Two hands on the milk.'

If either of us drops this, it's game over. This has to work and I'm sweating bullets like my life depends on it.

As careful as possible I slide Blackie into its slot. Closing my eyes, I take a deep breath. I exhale, then push down harder than I feel comfortable with, shooting a prayer heavenward.

I feel the click.

You can't hear it, but you can feel it. Every time I feel that slight click when it seats itself just right, I say to myself, 'Put that in your pipe and smoke it, MD! You vertigo loving, no good bastard!'

I won again.

Blackie's in, and if my bike turns on, I'm good to go. My bike lights up like it can't wait to get rolling, inviting me to climb on. Forty miles to go, and day one will be in the books.

Later, with all three of the team safely at the campsite, I call Dave for directions.

"Go into Anton and when you see the only

building, take a left and go a 1/4 mile. You'll see us on the right."

Perfect.

This would become one of my favorite parts of the day. Getting the phone call that says Bill found a place to stay and here's how you find it. A wave of relief washes over me each and every time. My anxiety drops. I have a final destination for the day. My mind eases and I mentally relax.

Dave:

So the last time I saw Steve was inside Denver city limits, and he was doing great. The weather was perfect and everyone was having a good time riding and chatting.

I was among the first to peel off from cycling since I had the important job of getting the support van out to Steve. Yeah, that meant all our supplies; everything to keep him and I alive (hopefully) for the next month.

We spoke on the phone as I neared the crossroads of Watkins, Colorado, and he still sounded great. He was upbeat and confident and I thought, "Well, good. This is going really well."

When Steve told me he wanted to do 100 miles on the first day, I tried countless times to talk him out of it. Why 100 miles on the first day? The math said that if we went at least 50 miles a day, we'd get to Columbus in a month. And if we did, say, 60-80 miles a day, we could be ahead of the curve and have a few days for rest, sickness or any unexpected issues like flat tires or replacing batteries.

Or even replacing a whole E-bike if we had to.

I was of the theory that if you gas yourself right out of the gate, you have less chance of making it to the finish. You can burn out too quickly. It only made sense that someone who hadn't been off the couch in years should pace himself. So I could not for the life of me make sense of the 100 mile goal.

Now, taking into account that I'd been with Steve maybe only slightly less than his own wife and kid since his diagnosis eight years ago—which includes seeing a full-blown vertigo attack—when I pulled up to him in Strasburg, Colorado, I'd never seen him look so bad. He was in the shade sitting with his head firmly cocked back against the cold brick of the post office. He looked as if he'd been run over by a truck and then someone took a shovel and discarded him in the grass.

No joke. He looked horrible.

I turned off the van, leaned back in my seat and thought, 'Oh my God. We're done before we even start.'

All the planning, donations, people watching, praying, willing and hoping . . . it poofed before my eyes. But if we had to stop now, it was OK because all that crap meant nothing compared to my brother's health and well-being. We'd live to fight another day. It'd be OK.

I got out of the van and immediately asked if he was OK and what did he need? I think my hand was hovering over 911 as I calculated where the nearest hospital might be and if I could get him there faster than an ambulance. He asked for some ice and a cold, soaked towel, which I got from the cooler. As he gingerly wrapped the towel around his neck I was debating in my head whether I might have to stop him if he didn't stop himself. To continue like this would be madness. Should I call someone? Could my dad get him to stop?

"I'll be ok, I just need to rest my head for a little while," he said.

I know keeping your head still is part of Ménière's. It gives your brain a break from having to deal with conflicting balance messages between the good ear and the one that's *off the rails.*

It's gotta be hell.

But I wait and see what he wants to do. He's been managing this for years, and I'm trying to stay calm and trust his judgement.

He asks, "Is there somewhere I can use the bathroom?"

I look down the street. "There's a gas station right down there. Do you think you can make it?"

He reached out and I pulled him up. Towel around his neck, we started off toward the gas station.

He's talking a little freer now; life seems to be pouring back into him as we walk. We got to the gas station and he used the bathroom and got a drink. After that he seemed totally fine and ready to go. I was pretty amazed, but glad and relieved. And somewhat shocked at the total transformation I'd just witnessed before my eyes.

We walked back to the van, switched the bike battery, and he was off again in good spirits. Great spirits, actually. I caught up to him and took a video of him sailing down the middle of Route 36 goofing around waving his arms going no-handed. I film, still amazed at what I just witnessed back in town.

Steve would tell me later that since he feels awful all the time, he doesn't grade on a curve. It's all bad to him, never good. So there's no gradient of bad to worse as you or I might think of it. That's part of the hell of having Ménière's.

And my education was only just beginning.

CHAPTER 5

In a town with a population of 126, it was a breeze finding the campground. Hell, more people live in my condo complex back home.

I take a left at the only building I see. It's a run down country store with old gas pumps out front. In another quarter mile I take a right into the Prairie Motel and Campground (not to be confused with Prairie Dog State Park in Norton, Kansas, that would come later). The camp is a barren wasteland. A cow pasture with not a tree in sight. There's a small motel and a giant field of nothing. But I love it just for the simple fact that I'm here.

It wasn't hard to find the guys, considering they were the only one's there. There's 50 campsites, but it was hard to distinguish one from another. The layout was haphazard at best. It was one big, empty field, simple as that.

When the guys checked-in to ask what spot we reserved, they were told with cheer and politeness, "Whichever one you want." There were a handful of RV spots, and I use that term loosely, but they did have RV hookups.

This would become a pattern for us. Finding campsites close to RV hookups so we could poach their 110 outlets to charge phones and especially my bike batteries. We discovered early on that my battery charged quicker in a hard-wired outlet compared to the trickle charge from the van's dash. But thank God the van had charger ability at all. That was huge for us.

They picked a spot (and, again, I use the term loosely) that was 30 feet from a 110 outlet. It was a rotted post, two foot tall with an outlet box dangling from one screw.

Perfect.

I quickly inspect my bike to see if there's any damage from the first day's pounding.

Having Bryce as a bike tech from his racing days was crucial; I would pick his brain often while he's with us. It also turns out he is a phenomenal cook! Who knew?

After Bill and I pitch our tents (Dave and Bryce would sleep in their vehicles), Bryce pulls out a cooking stove that fits perfectly on his tailgate. Before long he has whipped up the best double cheeseburgers I've ever eaten, hands down. Maybe it was because of the long stressful day, but those puppies were pure ecstasy!

Reclining in my camp chair resting with a full belly I take a few moments to look at this trip from the inside out. No longer can I daydream about what it will feel like. No more questioning my ability to ride 100 miles . . . or not. No more wondering what could go wrong. Now I was on the inside. I'd made it through the day, and survived. Sure, my adrenaline is still off the charts, but mentally I am spent.

At that moment my brain feels like I'm driving a car into a parking lot, putting it in park and crushing the pedal to the metal. But you're not moving as you rev the engine full-tilt watching the needle climb towards the red line. It's an odd feeling that's hard to explain. I'm talking too fast and too much, driving the team nuts. Eventually, I ease off my inner gas pedal and start to settle in.

Physical exhaustion is part of any chronic illness, but especially for us MD'ers. My brain has to differentiate all the mixed signals it receives, and it's maddening. My left ear tells my brain I'm upside down. My right ear says I'm right side up. What is my brain to do? Which ear should it believe? Dizziness is the outcome and it never takes a break.

Never.

I live carsick all the time. All. The. Time.

The only thing that helps is resting my head against something solid, be it a wall, a high back chair, or best case scenario, my couch. I always need to lay down with my head still. Always. That's the only time my brain gets relief from the confusion of which way is up. My body is at rest, so my head is at rest, so my brain is at rest. That's how it works.

As soon as I stand up . . . or move . . . the clowns fly out of the car and the ICBMs start misfiring in my head in a million directions at once.

It's maddening.

So a big part of the potential success of this trip is my Walmart camping chair. It's low to the ground and reclines back with a pillow-like headrest. After a couple minutes in my chair, and really, immediately any time I flop down in it, I start to feel more settled. The clowns get back in the car and the ICBMs stop firing.

We sit around well past dark, drinking beer, telling stories, and making fun of each other. We laugh—several times to the point of tears. It feels great. I know I have to get up tomorrow and do it all over again, but today was a great day. It truly was.

For now we bask in our small victory. I stop questioning my stupidity and start looking forward to the next day.

I'm doing this for everyone who is haunted by a chronic illness, be it Ménière's or something else. For all who have a monster trying to suck them down. It's not a competition of who's the sickest. Everyone has some burden to carry. For one month I'm hoping to carry mine with dignity and without shame. As I crawl into my tent and wrestle into my sleeping bag, I lift my left hand, stick a middle finger in the air as one last salute to the MD

37

Monster. 'Not today! Try again tomorrow, you sick bastard!'

And if all goes well tomorrow, I'll be in Kansas.

Eight years before this trip I attended my friend Amy's 40th birthday party. I remember it well because that's the night my life changed forever. I stood in the kitchen among 15 other people. The atmosphere was festive and joyous. Music was playing, drinks were being consumed and people were mingling in every corner of the three bedroom condo.

Standing in the kitchen, beer in hand, I caught up with friends I hadn't seen in a while. Suddenly my left ear started ringing.

The music faded and my friend's mouths were moving but I felt like I'd slipped into a vacuum. I looked around to see if anyone else was hearing what I was hearing. To my dismay and confusion, it quickly became apparent the loud metallic screech was all mine.

I excused myself and went out the back door onto the deck. I needed to escape the sensation I was feeling. All the voices and music and sounds of people moving was over-whelming. It felt like there were five stereos playing different songs at the same volume simultaneously. I couldn't differentiate one sound from another. I lost all concentration and was hoping some fresh air on the back deck would alleviate the sensation.

I collapsed into a patio chair, looked around at all the people and couldn't make out their conversations. I had to turn my head sideways and use all of my concentration to understand what was being said.

It's been like that ever since.

That was the first punch thrown by the Monster and it landed solid. Like Muhammad Ali tagging Joe Frazier square on the jaw, it was a game-changer. But this particular blow was permanent. I couldn't shake my head loose of the wooziness like a boxer could. I couldn't rub dirt on it or walk it off.

In a split-second, I became disabled.

PART 2

Kansas: 1st overture

Anton, Colorado-St. Francis, Kansas, 96 miles
St. Francis, Kansas-Norton, Kansas, 107 miles

CHAPTER 6

September 2, 2020

Day Two

We pack up camp as the sun rises over a perfectly flat horizon. I gather my belongings, roll up my sack, and jam my tent into its bag.

It's only day two and we haven't figured out the perfect system for what goes where in the van. But Dave is very organized. I know he will become efficient. A few days later he would have this down to a science. After all, this is his space; it's where he works.

I am focused on riding my bike. That's my only job today, as it would be everyday.

Our friend Bryce rolls, literally out of his truck, looking fresh as the noonday sun. Unlike myself, Bryce was, and still is, an avid cyclist. He and Dave would take turns riding the first few miles of my day and sometimes the last few miles. I loved this because they were both healthy and active and keeping up with my E-bike wasn't an issue. I set a pace I was comfortable with and they followed on my wing. Never once did either tell me to slow down or speed up. And I love them for it. I respect that they let me do what I needed to do to get through my day.

Back in the planning stage, Emily and I had decided St. Francis, Kansas, would be my goal for today. In retrospect, I'm thankful for the evening we spent on the couch plotting my course and destinations. Our team had no idea where we would camp each night, but we did know our target town. This proved helpful because with four people doing four different things, at least we all knew where we would end up.

Once packed this morning, I open the van's side doors and sit on the lip. This would become a daily routine for me. At the end of day one, I had haphazardly crammed my waist-pack and the shirt off my back into the window-well of the passenger-side dashboard. Again, the van was Dave's space. But once we were done for the day he relinquished the entire passenger seat area to me. This was where I put my backpack and other necessities for easy access during the evening.

Most of the time the front area was also Dave's mobile office. Equipped with 110 outlets and a few USB jacks, we were always charging something. A laptop, one to three phones, my portable charging brick, and/or my headphones. The dash resembled NASA Control in Houston, and I'm sure we could make a few storm chasers jealous.

With the van, like me with my tent, we each found a system where we always took things out and put them back exactly in the same place. You had to, or you ended up spending large amounts of time simply trying to find whatever the hell you needed in that moment. It quickly became maddening, so we had no option but to practice extreme organization.

As I said, I was so tired that first night I simply took everything and jammed it in the passenger-side window well. This worked so well I repeated it for the next 24 days. I didn't want to wake up and have to hunt around for my knee brace (20 years ago I blew out my MCL snowboarding so I wore a brace as a precaution), or look around for other things like my headphones or other essentials. My goal was to get up and get going. I'd grab my pile of crap off the dash, sit on the stoop of the van and get ready.

Eventually I got this process down to under 10 minutes.

Bryce and I finally take off around 7:30 a.m. He'll ride with me as far as he likes, then turn back to leap-frog his truck to the next camp. I checked the weather last night and it looked like it was going to warm up over the next four days. If I could get most of my miles in before noon I could avoid the hottest part of the day. I push off—Day Two!—with a little wobble until I find my balance. Bryce is right behind me.

Dave is filming and yells, "Good luck!"

Bill yells, "Bryce, push him hard!" which I didn't hear, but ironically right after I can be heard on video saying, "Bryce, I'm not going to push it hard today," and Bryce nods.

So we've finally left the campground, passed four giant grain silos with sunbeams stabbing through like swords, and we head out once again on Route 36.

Bryce tells me he wants to ride 15 miles before turning around. I think to myself, idiot, doesn't he know that's 30 miles round trip back to his truck? Then I remember that's a walk in the park for a guy who actually rides bikes.

CHAPTER 7

Bryce turns around after 15 miles looking fresh as a daisy. We say our goodbyes and without missing a rotation, I keep going. I'd see him this evening in St. Francis . . . if I can make it.

After showering (not together), Dave and Bill shopped for supplies at a small country store nearby. Bryce rolled up and gave them a favorable report of our morning ride. I call Dave and tell him I'm going to need a battery switch soon. Looking at his hard-copy Rand McNally map (yep, old-school . . . respect) he says the town of Idelia looks good. I say okay and keep battling.

The cross winds are becoming more and more ferocious, making it hell to keep a straight line. Traffic is sparse though, and I'm feeling good. At one point I round a bend and find myself surrounded on both sides by endless fields of sunflowers. I'm so taken aback by the beauty I drop my headset mic and call my Mom. I wish she could experience this, and I want to share this moment with her. It was like being in the land of Oz. It felt magical. Corn and soybeans were all I'd seen for many miles now, so this change of scenery is a shock and I welcome it. I need to share it with someone.

Upon arriving in Idelia (I can't call it a town per se because it was smaller than Anton, which was damn-near non-existent) I see the van and Harley parked up ahead on the left. They're in front of an ice cream shop/gas station/feed store. I tell them the wind is beating me up pretty good but I feel like I can make it to St. Francis.

Kansas is not known for its forests, so shade was at a minimum. I need shade. I love shade. The heat wasn't too bad today but I still looked forward to resting in my camp chair . . . in the shade.

After I cruise into the gas station/ice cream parlor/feed store, Dave grabs an ice cream cone, Bill and I switch my battery and I eat a banana while sitting in my chair. Bryce pulls up shortly thereafter in his truck. I know my potassium level is low. Don't ask me how, I can just feel it. I take a daily diuretic to flush salt from my system. This also depletes my potassium level.

Salt is my enemy. It inflames the fluid in my ear causing many issues, and none of them are good. A normal body knows how to balance salt and what it does to the inner ear. Mine, not so much. My inner ear becomes inflamed which causes pressure to build that my body can't regulate. Too much salt makes me violently ill. Major nausea and possible full-on vertigo attacks can occur.

A low salt diet, which consists of 1,500 mg a day or less is important for me to manage my disease. While my meds help flush salt from my system, it also flushes potassium.

Bananas are a great source of potassium, but I hate them. You have no idea how much I hate them! But now I have a decision to make: To banana or not to banana, that is the question. But I quickly decide if I'm going to be successful on this trip, I and the banana will have to make peace. I'll have to start eating them.

As the guys look on taking joy and delight in my anguish, I choke one down like I'm chewing a dog turd. But I feel better instantly. To this day I still force one down each day, so go figure. I guess you can get used to anything if you have no choice and it makes you feel better.

I get up from my chair as Bill fires up the Harley and says his battery is on its last legs. "I'm going to have to get it replaced. I don't think I can go another day," he says.

Dave and I exchange worried looks. Where the hell will he find a motorcycle battery out here? Most of these towns are too small to have an apple and a can of Coke.

Bill and Bryce decide to race on up to St. Francis to shop for a battery and start scouting for a place to camp. Dave hangs back for an hour or two to give me a head-start while he works on social media.

Dave has a journalism degree from The Ohio State University and has written for major newspapers. He's also been an IT guy, and has done computer work and journalism in Italy and the Middle East. But editing and posting social media videos is something he's learning by the seat of his pants. He's spending hours chasing the learning curve and this whole endeavor would not have happened without his energy and focus. I am the face of the trip, but he is the backbone and I owe him a lifetime's amount of gratitude.

We are posting a couple times a day on Facebook and Instagram, so Dave has the laborious weight of filming and editing all of our videos. Neither of us had an Instagram account until four days before we left. We created a Facebook page, Instagram account, and a GoFundMe site all on the fly in a matter of weeks, *and* we had to learn how to use them.

Yeah, it was a lot.

But we did it.

And not without me peppering my 18-year-old son, Nolan, and my wife, Emily, with questions out the Ying-Yang on a nearly hourly basis.

So I eventually take off from the ice cream/gas station/feed store and an hour later Dave passes me just in time to film me crossing the border from Colorado into Kansas. He soon passes me again with flashers flashing, rolling slowly enough to see my thumbs-up (a routine we'd repeat many times each day) then disappears over the horizon.

I'm alone again and fighting a massive headwind.

I thought traveling west to east would give me tailwinds, but with the recent hurricane activity in the southeast, the weather was pushing everything toward me. The headwinds are excruciating but I've accomplished getting into the next state and this gives me a mental boost. I think I'm going to make it to St. Francis. It's just going to take ten hours.

I glide into some sort of eerie dream-state when suddenly the phone in my right pocket vibrates. I pull it out, hit the red pulsing picture of a phone, and pull my headset mic down. It's Dave. We've found a campsite and here's how to get there.

Like I said before, I love getting these calls. I start to imagine it: me in my camp chair, my tent set up, relaxing. Because of the headwind, this has been a long 96 miles. And I'm ready to rest.

CHAPTER 8

The campsite is great. For one, it's free. I turn right at the St. Francis fire station, go down a gravel road and into what looks like a town park. It has concrete shelters, a bathroom facility and most importantly, electric RV hookups.

Score.

There's no one else in the entire place, save for one couple, so we have our pick of spots. We spread out under some trees, the first I've seen all day. Bill works on his bike battery while I set up my tent. Having shade is the best part.

The worst part is realizing we're camping 200 yards from the city compost dump. Right on the other side of our narrow row of trees is a pile of smelly garbage. Trucks roll in every 15 minutes or so to add to this smelly pile of shit. And with that comes the flies. The dump is a breeding ground for those little bastards, and they bite you. So we all take showers in bug spray as Bryce sets up his cookstove. We may as well have set up camp in the dump itself.

It probably doesn't help that though Bryce and Dave went to the store to get brats and hotdogs, they came back with steaks. I love that they brought back steaks because I need a protein boost, and the guys found a manager's special at the local market. But with the wind racing in the wrong direction, people in Colorado 50 miles behind us can probably smell the steaks cooking. And so does every goddamned fly between here and there.

That sweet, beautiful aroma of roasting cow flesh wafts through the compost dump causing a Discovery-Channel Shark-Week-like feeding frenzy of flies on steak the likes of which I've never seen before. But armed with my shower of bug spray, I'm so grateful to be done riding and have a comfortable place to camp that I don't mind sharing my steak with half a billion flies.

C'est la vie.

I'm not a tech wiz, and neither is my brother as far as what we were doing, but when our social media began picking up followers, another part of my daily routine became trying to touch base with as many people as possible.

If someone commented on one of our sites, I did my best to thank them or give a quick comment in return.

That was important to me because I truly appreciated anyone willing to take the time to follow our trip.

Each night after crawling into my orange bubble tent, as I call it now, I spent an hour or more scrolling what Dave posted that day and did my best to catch up with the comments.

Sleep does not come easily with tinnitus (ringing in the ear), so I needed a distraction till exhaustion overtook me and my brain gave up battling to decipher the cacophony in my head.

Once finished with social media, I would normally turn on a baseball game. I love baseball, but if anything can put you to sleep faster than a jackrabbit tied to a cannon ball it's a baseball broadcast. So my nights were quickly finding a pattern, too. The orange bubble was becoming my safe place, my bat cave. It wasn't my bed at home, but I liked having my own space.

After a good night's sleep, the next morning I pack up my tent and grab my gear off the dash in the van. This would be my morning routine from here on out.

To my chagrin, and more to Dave's, the van is filled

with flies. Some have even hitched a ride all the way from Anton. There must have been a minimum of 50 flies buzzing around the inside of the van. Some even rode shotgun with Dave all the way to the border of Missouri, for God's sakes.

Bug bites would become a regular nuisance for me. I wore flip-flops and shorts each evening and after just two nights I have bites up and down each arm with chigger bites all over my feet and ankles. The fly-bites hurt for a while but the chigger bites itch for days. I'd never get used to that. When I ask the other guys if they're as bitten to death as I am, they shake their heads.

Hmmm. Maybe my poop and pee treks into farmer's fields is where I'm picking up the extra insect attention?

Anyway, Bryce is again riding the first 15 miles with me this morning. Today's destination: the town of Norton, Kansas—107 miles if all goes well.

It didn't.

I strap my gear on, ready to go. I know I have a long day ahead of me, but I have water, snacks, music and I'm praying for no headwinds.

Wrong.

We pedal up the gravel road toward Route 36. We pass the fire station on our right. We make a right turn and head east. POW!

Immediately the wind hits us like Sammy Sosa swinging a home run straight into my chest.

"Goddammit!" I yell out loud, but Bryce doesn't hear me.

The wind is howling.

Absolutely howling.

Even with the electric assist I am working hard. I can't imagine how Bryce feels pedaling a normal bike. One mile down the road I feel anxiety coming over me.

The thought of doing what I did yesterday all over again begins to overwhelm me. I know the feeling of extreme anxiety well and it's paralyzing. But I try to put it out of my mind and concentrate on surviving the wind.

I think back to conversations Dave and I had about social media before we left. We wanted people to follow the trip, but I knew my part had to be real, raw, and informative. I'd made the conscious decision to pull the curtain back, and I let Dave know I wanted everything filmed: the good, the bad, and the ugly.

Everything.

In 'real' life people mostly see me only on my good days, or when I can get out of bed, or make a phone call. What people don't see are the hours upon hours and days upon days where I suffer alone. And there was no reason to do this trip for awareness and fundraising if I was unwilling to be transparent.

A mile and a quarter down the road, I ask Bryce to pull over. "Can you get out your phone and start videoing?" I ask.

To Bryce's credit he doesn't get worried or start asking questions. He doesn't know I'm on the precipice of an important decision; another first: Am I willing to let everyone see me as a weak person? A person who suffers. A person that comes apart at the seams?

As Bryce raises his phone, I think to myself, 'If you're not willing to be real, you're a chickenshit and should turn around now and call this whole thing off.'

And I meant it.

As cars and trucks whiz by, Bryce stands on the side of the road filming every second of my emotional breakdown. When I'm done I tell him I want this posted as soon as he gets back to camp. He says he will and I'm grateful for his patience and agreement. I'm sure he's rattled.

We get back on our bikes and Bryce rides out his 15 miles. As he turns back I tell him I'm fine and I'll see y'all down the road.

Bryce goes back to St. Francis to meet up with the guys at a coffee shop. It would be four hours before I would need to switch batteries so they could relax, get some breakfast and visit the motorcycle museum in town. I heard Bill mention the museum last night and knew he was excited to go.

Dave:

Even with all the flies, St. Francis was a really fun stay. After Bill and Bryce took care of Bill's battery debacle, they went to a local liquor store where they had a jovial chat with the young woman behind the counter. They told her about the trip and she agreed to put up one of our flyers in the window (we made flyers for our trip to pass out as we went, since, after all, this was a trip about fundraising and awareness).

Later on that evening Bryce and I decided to take a nice, relaxing bike cruise through town and took pictures of ourselves among prominent features.

It was great.

Things were going awesome so far.

In the middle of the night, I awoke to my van shaking as if there were people outside rocking it back and forth.

'What the hell . . . ?' I wondered in my fog.

I laid there for a moment and it happened again. The van was violently rocking side to side.

'That . . . can't be the wind, can it?'

But it was.

A wind unlike anything I'd ever experienced. It eventually went from violent to just a gentle shake rocking me back to sleep like a baby. But not before the thought

55

crossed my mind: *Steve and Bill are out there in tents! Or at least what'd be left of them.*

I fully expected them to be jumping in the van any second, but they never did.

The next morning was still windy, but not like last night. "Did you guys feel that wind last night?" I asked the gang.

They said, yeah, their tents pretty much flattened against them all night, but they managed to sleep through it.

"I don't see how you could . . . "

Wind or no wind, Steve looked horrible. As bad as he'd looked at the post office before Anton. Maybe worse. "Are you ok?"

He stood for a moment on the verge of tears. And then tears. Bill and I walked over to him. "I'll be alright," he choked out.

Bill put a hand on his shoulder. "Are you alright? Do you want to sit down? Rest today? Whatever you need."

"No, I'm going to go. Just need a minute."

He was sobbing and we felt helpless. Though I didn't agree with doing 100 miles the first day, I certainly would've thought he would take it easy the second day.

He didn't.

Before going to bed in Anton, he announced, "Well, another 100 mile day tomorrow." I was like, What? Seemed strange to me not to do a 30–60 mile day the second day. But he busted out another 100 miles. And again, last night before bed, "Another 100 miles tomorrow." And again, I was like, 'What? Why? Three 100 mile days in a row to start? What are we trying to do out here? Kill ourselves or make it across the country?'

I didn't understand, but Steve was undeterred. And now that he was crumbling into what seemed to me an exhausted mess, I couldn't understand the logic of what was happening. But Bill got him stabilized and he assured us he'd be all right, so he and Bryce eventually shoved off.

With the boys on the road, Bill and I found a coffee shop in town and ordered some eggs. As we were eating, Bryce came in frantic looking like he'd seen a ghost.

"Are you OK?" I asked.

"Well, Steve's in bad shape and he had me take a video and wants you to post it right away," he said.

As Bill and I watched the video, our spirits sank.

I looked at Bryce, "Oh my God. What happened out there?"

"He was really bad. The wind was brutal. It was killing us both. But I didn't know if I should pull him off the bike."

Poor Bryce. I knew he didn't know Steve well enough to feel comfortable stopping him. But I knew he raced back to me and Bill because hopefully we did. I posted the video to social media and the three of us discussed whether we should stop Steve for the day.

And what if he resisted?

Should we override him?

Could/should we physically pull him off the bike if that's what it came to?

I decided to call him.

"Did you post the video?" he asked right away.

"Yeah, are you OK out there?"

"It's tough but I'm making it. The headwind is killing me."

He sounded OK enough to dissipate my worry, and assured me he could continue.

"I'll tell you if I need to stop," he said, and gave us a time frame to meet him for a battery switch.

"Ok, well, we're going to see the motorcycle museum if you're good for the moment."

"I'm OK, go see the museum then catch up to me."

When we did catch up to him, he explained to us (and to me again) that every day was a bad day for him. The way he felt that morning wasn't any different than any other day.

"If I go to the grocery store, this is what I feel like; this is what my life is like," he said. "If I ride 100 miles on my bike, this is what life is like. It's all the same to me. It's all suffering no matter what I'm doing, unless I'm on my couch. It's just that most people don't see me on a daily basis like this, as you guys are doing now."

Again, this was our education in Ménière's, and again, we were slowly getting it. We trusted what he told us and the ride continued.

On to the next town.

CHAPTER 9

I was crying in the social media clip we posted that morning, my nose was running and I talked about suffering and being broken. It looked like a complete emotional breakdown. But to me, it was no big deal. It was like looking at a reflection of my real life in a still pond.

This was the real me.

But if you don't live with a chronic illness that steals everything you love doing, and gives you no other option but to simply survive, then I can understand how scary this might look. To me, it was just another day with the Monster. Sure, he found a crack in my armor this morning, but that's the reason we in the Ménière's community call ourselves 'Warriors.' It's our battle cry to not give up. It's our way to say, 'You're a fighter, so keep fighting. You will suffer, but don't let it get the best of you.'

As I am riding, I know the exact second the social media post blows up. I have my phone set to 'alert notifications,' so as I am trying to concentrate in the wind and somewhat enjoy 'Pour Some Sugar On Me,' the dings become rapid and unrelenting.

On the one hand, people with Ménière's are encouraging me: "Stay strong, you got this, keep pedaling you're doing great." On the other, the non-Ménière's community hits from a different angle: "Maybe you should stop! You look sick and emotionally unstable."

Well, no shit, Sherlock. Welcome to MY world. I am sick and I'm always on the emotional edge. Sorry I'm having a bad day, but this is most of my days. No one gets to see me like this because it's embarrassing. Would I rather be at home in bed? Hell, yes! But not this month.

This month I'm exposing my reality. I'm exposing the Monster. But in the midst of people posting and questioning my sanity, I read many comments later that were super encouraging.

Without a doubt, the team was struggling with tough decisions to make. If they decided at any point to pull me off my bike and I resisted, would they physically pull me off? Bryce would tell me later he and his wife Isabel had this discussion before the trip and decided, 'If you have to stop him, stop him even if you have to drag him kicking and screaming into the truck.'

But the team agreed to see how I was doing when they caught up to me. Of course they were all in agreement, 'If we have to stop him, it's three against one.'

I'm sitting on the side of the road when Dave is the first to pull up. I'd taken off my bright yellow safety vest and I'm sitting on it. I'm on a slight downslope off the shoulder in the grass. I left my bike on the shoulder so Dave wouldn't miss me. We swap batteries and Dave expresses his concern.

This was also a defining moment for us. I tell him "I understand the concern you have, as well as the team, but I'm okay to ride. I promise I will tell you if I need to stop and can't go on. I promise. You need to trust me on this. I know myself and this ain't shit. Just another bad day like thousands before."

I was sure he was feeling pressure, especially after the video he posted that morning. But we talk some more and Dave says, "Ok, I trust you to be honest about how you're doing."

It was a defining moment because it built the trust we needed in order to succeed. Every day after that he let me ride if I said I could. And true to my word, there would be days I did call and say I can't go anymore today, come and get me.

Eventually he takes off and I ride the next four hours until the second battery swap.

The whole team meets at a crossroads gas station for what we hope is the last battery swap of the day. We're twenty miles short of our destination of Norton, Kansas, and it's been a hella long day. Not only had the wind kicked my ass, but now it was hot as balls.

I'd been rolling over steep flowing hills for most of the day when I crest a long hill to see two figures on bikes rolling toward me in the distance. 'What are those assholes doing?' I think, incredulous. 'Who'd be stupid enough to be riding out here on a day like this?'

Then I realize it's Bryce and Dave, happily cruising toward me with the tailwind doppelganger of my hellish headwind. I relax once again, and we ride and chat down the hill to the gas station where Bill awaits.

Bryce informs me he booked a campsite at the Prairie Dog State Park in Norton earlier in the day and I'm excited at the news. As we pull into the gas station, I spot the van. 'Twenty miles left today,' I say to myself as I pull up. 'And the Monster is once again conquered.'

I roll to a stop behind Bill's motorcycle and Dave says, "You got to hear this." Apparently when Dave and Bryce pulled into the gas station side by side, Dave thought they might be in handicap spaces. But the spaces weren't marked clearly and, besides, the gas station was empty. The roads were empty. There was no one around. So Dave and Bryce parked, rolled down windows, and began talking to each other.

That's when Dave heard a voice and saw a head down below Bryce's driver side window. "Don't worry about me, you go ahead and park there!"

Bryce immediately pulls out of the space and Dave

61

realizes it was a guy in an *actual* wheelchair suddenly giving Bryce crap because he can't get up the ramp.

They had, indeed, parked in handicap spaces, and for the first time ever, in a gas station in the middle of nowhere, having pulled in with not another human being in sight for hundreds, if not thousands, of miles, they had blocked a poor handicapped man in a wheelchair from getting up the handicap ramp.

It was hilarious.

You couldn't have scripted it better for a movie.

And yet, it turned out the wheelchair man had a sense of humor, and he and Bill became good friends while Bryce and Dave took off to meet me.

So all's well that ends well.

And after what had been a monumentally stressful day for all of us, we needed a good laugh. (The fact it came at Bryce's expense made it even funnier. He's the nicest guy in the world.)

After a short rest in the shade and what I'd hope will be our last battery swap of the day (God, please let it be the last!) I bend over, kiss my bike for luck, turn to Bill on his Harley, take a deep breath and say "Fuck."

Bill laughs knowing I'd given it all I had today. His laugh encourages me. He understands me, and I know he wants me to keep fighting.

The wind did die down a bit but the last 20 miles of each day always hits me the hardest. Mentally I'm already in my chair, my tent set up, and at rest. But 20 miles on a bike is still one and a half to two hours of riding. It's never easy and always a mental dick punch.

Dave rings me up on my headset an hour and a half later. This is the moment I've waited for. "We're at the campsite but it's too difficult to explain how to get here. So I'll meet you at the ranger station at the entrance off

Route 36 and you can follow me back from there."

I arrive at the ranger station, park the bike, sit down against a wood fence and wait for Dave to drive up from the campsite. From where I sit, it's all downhill, and to our surprise and relief there is a lake, and we are camped right next to it.

When Dave pulls up, I tell him I want to make another video. I knew the video from that morning had caused a wave of concern on social media and I wanted to show I was doing okay, Ménière's couldn't keep me down, so up yours Ménière's! Dave sends the video, fires up the van and we start the crazy traverse down toward the campsite.

The state park was perfect and best of all, the place was empty. It felt so good there I soon told the guys to book another night and we'd take tomorrow off.

Chef Bryce once again cooks up a masterful dinner. Tonight it's brats and hotdogs.

We relax and enjoy each other's company once again. We make fun of Dave for blowing out—not one, but two—tires on Bryce's borrowed bike while riding around a park where we'd had lunch. Then we revisit Bryce and the wheelchair guy. We make fun of Bill, because, well, he's Bill. He can dish it, but can also take it. We are all feeling pretty good as the sun begins to set.

But we're also a bit sad because it's Bryce's last day. He's scheduled to cruise home tonight for his daughter's birthday party the next day. So around 9 p.m., we make a thank you video with Bryce for social media and he fires up his truck for home. Selfish bastard, leaving us. Just kidding. He was a great part of the team and it's hard to see him go.

But before he left he made sure to teach me the basics of bike maintenance. How to lube the chain and how often, things like that which would prove invaluable in the days ahead. I knew nothing about bikes so I was sure my ignorance was killing him. I don't use toe clip-ins or wear bicycle clothes. I do wear gel shorts because 1,400 miles is a lot of punishment on the bum, but on my head nothing but a bandana or ball cap. It's as if I were riding to my neighborhood corner store and forgot to stop. I have no interest in being aerodynamic. My bike's not made for speed, it's made for comfort. After just three days it already feels like a part of me. Like it just grew out of my butt or something.

But to be truthful, my ass was starting to hurt from the punishment. Each morning, and every battery switch I would drop trow and load my britches with baby powder. It helped somewhat, but my butt was sore from day one till day 25.

With Bryce gone the team is now down to three.

Tonight's RV hookups are quite a ways away and up a fairly steep hill, but we have all day tomorrow to worry about that. Two RVs pull in late that night and we watch as they set up shop up the hill. These are our only neighbors and I'm looking forward to hanging out here all day tomorrow.

After crawling into my tent and checking social media, I turn on a ballgame and begin drifting off to sleep. But not before raising a middle finger with a smile. 'Not today you assbag Ménière's piece of shit, not today.'

"It should go away in a couple days," my family physician told me. "I don't see anything wrong with your eardrums, but it wouldn't hurt to flush your ears out."

"Will it fix me?" I asked. It's been a week since the party, and the ringing hasn't stopped. Not for a second.

"It might, it might not, but it can't hurt," he replied.

A nurse entered and sprayed hot water in each of my ears to break up the wax buildup. She held a silver metal bowl under my ear to catch the debris. I gagged a little when I saw the earwax soup we'd created. To my surprise, my hearing actually improved a bit but the noise didn't go away. "Oh shit," I squeaked out. "I hope this isn't permanent."

At the time I thought there had to be something that would make this annoying sound go away. There just had to be.

"Here's a business card for an ENT in Vail," my physician graciously offered. "If the ringing doesn't stop you should go see him."

Jesus! A specialist? 'This can't be that serious,' I thought to myself. Just make the ringing go away so I can have my hearing back. I'm sure there's a simple solution; a pill, a treatment, something! No one can live like this forever, that's impossible!

Two weeks later I made an appointment with the ENT.

The ENT ran a few tests and told me I

have tinnitus. It's permanent, it won't go away. "Here's a prescription for some steroids," he said. "Not a cure but it might help alleviate the inflammation a little."

WTF? The only word I heard was 'permanent.' That was eight years ago, and here we are. Still ringing. And not only that, but dizziness, constant carsickness and oh, yeah, the funnest one of all, random vertigo attacks, have been added to the mix.

Son of a bitch.

The only word I heard was 'permanent.'

PART 3

Kansas: Second Overture

Norton, Kansas-Mankato, Kansas, 110 miles
Mankato, Kansas-Marysville, Kansas, 96 miles

CHAPTER 10

3 a.m., September 5th, 2020

Day Five

I take a right onto Route 36, after tracking back to the campsite to get the battery.

I'm almost through the town of Norton when I spot the diner on the left where we had breakfast yesterday. It was the perfect midwest greasy spoon—old carpet, old tables, worn-out chairs, and a ceiling stained with years of grease and cigarette smoke permanently baked into the rectangle panels above. This place hasn't been updated since World War II, and it was perfect.

Exactly my kind of eatery.

Each morning I pounded a Gatorade to replenish my electrolytes. I'd also down an 8 oz. spicy V-8 to get my vegetables and my 480 mg. of salt to start the day. This is all I can usually stomach in the morning and it usually holds me over till dinner. I do snack throughout the day, but nothing substantial. While riding I'd normally eat a peanut butter sandwich and a handful of jerky every 30 miles. I'd also drink two bottles of water. That makes 40 oz. of water total, every 30 miles.

Since yesterday was our first day off, we decided to find a lazy diner, take down a big breakfast and head back to camp to rest. Our waitress Amy took our orders, sauntered toward the kitchen, and I blew my nose on a paper napkin.

I didn't want my snot rag on the table for the duration of our meal so I got up in search of a trash can. I wandered around a minute and spotted the restrooms on the far side of the restaurant. I headed that direction.

The only other patrons besides us were at a round six top table next to the restroom hallway. There were four women and a man at the table, the youngest would admit to being 73 years old.

Knowing a trash can awaited in the men's room, I passed their table and headed down the hallway. The restroom door was locked. Damn. The women's restroom was cracked open a bit. It was dark inside. I stood a second looking confused trying to decide if I should pop in. The problem was, I was five feet from the table of elderly coffee drinkers, and I didn't want to offend anyone. The closest lady, bless her heart, read my mind and told me go on in, we won't knock. I popped a foot inside and tossed my napkin in the wastebasket near the toilet.

As I passed the coffee club, I said, "I thought you guys were going to knock." We all laughed and I felt completely at ease.

"You're not from around here are you," the same lady smirked.

Norton has a population of 2,768 and I assume everyone knows everyone. On top of that, I haven't bathed or changed my clothes in four days. Other than changing my underwear, I'm still wearing my clothes from Denver—black shorts, white Modelo t-shirt, socks with a bucking horse and cowboy, and arm-sleeves with skulls to keep warm in the morning.

I've never been superstitious, but I do believe if it ain't broke, don't fix it. The clothes on my back had gotten me over 300 miles so why tempt fate by changing anything now?

It suddenly hit me that this group of elderly coffee drinkers probably thought I was a homeless hobo wandering in from the big city. "Yes ma'am," I told her politely. "I'm not a local." They looked me up and down, more from morbid curiosity than disgust probably. I told them I was riding a bike from Denver to Columbus, Ohio, to raise awareness for a rare disease I had.

They all nodded slowly, their heads bobbing in unison.

Another lady chimed, "Oh yes, I saw you pull up on your motorcycle." I told them that it was my friend's motorcycle, I was actually riding an E-bike. Apparently in rural Kansas an E-bike sighting is equivalent to the Space Shuttle landing on Main Street. This information heightened their curiosity, and they invited me to sit with them.

They wanted to hear all about this new-fangled E-bike and the trip I was on. After ten minutes we were best friends. Amy walked over to inform me that my breakfast had been on the table awhile.

"Can I bring it to you here?" she asked, nice as can be.

"No, I'll get to it in a bit, but thanks," I replied.

She said she would reheat it for me later if I wanted.

Damn, people are nice in Kansas. What the hell was this place, anyway?

An hour in I knew everything there was to know about the coffee club: Their kids' names, their grandchildren's names and what price corn was going for this season. In turn, they now knew all about my wife and son, my brother Dave, and our friend Bill with the Harley. I felt like I'd become a new member of their club. They told me they met there every day, seven days a week from 9 to 10:30 a.m.

I told them about my disease, and each one was sympathetic and understanding. I told them I'd be riding past tomorrow at 9 a.m. I asked if they'd be willing to come out and take a picture with me tomorrow as I pass by? They promised they'd be there and I promised to stop in, say hello/goodbye and take a picture.

Before I left, each one donated to my trip with fives, tens, and twenties. I did not solicit donations, so this meant the world to me.

Not once on the trip did I ask for donations, but if people wanted to donate, I accepted graciously. Times were tough right then with the COVID pandemic and all, so it was extremely humbling when anyone wanted to part with their hard earned cash.

That was when I realized the trip was going to mean something, that it would matter. That I wasn't just out here wasting my time. Until then I was in a bubble trying to survive the first three days.

Now the cat was out of the bag.

Meeting people and telling them my story would become a huge part of the trip from that day forward.

After handing them a couple flyers I returned to my table and scarfed down an ice cold breakfast.

But it couldn't have tasted better.

CHAPTER 11

I pedal past the diner at 3 a.m.

A wave of guilt nearly knocks me off my bike. I broke my promise. Shit. I promised to be at the diner at 9 a.m. to say good-bye and take pictures. But now I was gliding past and the coffee club wouldn't be arriving for another six hours.

'Man, I suck,' I think as the diner fades into the darkness behind me.

The people I would meet on this trip were a major reason I was out here. The bike ride was merely a platform, the people I'd meet were the real reason I was doing this.

And I just failed the first test.

Ménière's tends to make a person selfish. I do what I have to do to survive each day. At home in bed, selfishness hardly matters, but now I was putting myself in the public eye. So it was different. I'd let those people down. I silently apologize to the members of the coffee club of Norton as the diner disappears in my mirror. I feel like a schmuck. I hope they can forgive me.

The town of Norton itself soon disappears and once again I'm riding straight arrow east. Because of my insomnia I've been awake for more than 20 hours. By the time I'd sleep next, it'd be just under 48.

Mankato, Kansas, is the day's goal. It is 110 miles away, and leaving at 2:30 a.m. gave me a huge head start.

There's a chill in the air but it feels good. Not being able to see my surroundings, though, is unreal. I can't see the farms or cornfields as they go by. I don't see the horizon or anything that gives me a sense of space and time. It's just me, my bike, and whatever my narrow beam of light illuminates.

I'm not in the mood for my usual music. A metal-head at heart, I usually pick my favorite bands from the 80s or 90s to pass the time. But tonight it seems sacrilegious. The atmosphere is somber and still. This called for something atmospheric. I punch up Spotify as I ride and find a smooth jazz channel.

Perfect.

'Kind of Blue' from Miles Davis is just what I need. I haven't seen a car in over an hour and thankfully the bugs have thinned out since the lake back at Prairie Dog.

I apply my brakes and slow to a stop. I flip the kickstand down with my right foot and stand my bike in the middle of the road. I twist the handlebars just so, and sit down on the cool asphalt to make a 55-second video.

The headlight on my bike illuminates my face and it is eerie. But I feel I need to post a video to keep everyone up to date and want to capture the moment. Everyone should take time to drive to the middle of rural Kansas and sit in the middle of the road at 4 a.m. It's otherworldly.

Hours later as the sun is rising I pull into the town of Phillipsburg. I learned from working on a golf course in Colorado that the coldest time of day was the seconds right before the sun came up. Scientifically I don't know why that is. Seems counterintuitive to me. But it's true. So the half-hour before sunup brings a bone chill.

I spot the courthouse in the town square and sit on a bench. It's like being in a movie from the 50s. I can hardly wait for the sun to crest the shorter buildings to warm me up. In the meantime I enjoy a peanut butter sandwich and some jerky. I drink 20 oz. of water and look at the map on my phone.

Since it was such a peaceful night, I hadn't been pushing myself too hard. I really enjoyed riding at night and wanted to immerse myself in the experience. I was behind my normal pace, but what else did I have to do for the rest of the day? I realized I needed to enjoy my experience more. And on that park bench with the sun soon warming my face, I decide to chill the fuck out a little.

I'm halfway to Mankato and the sun is just rising. I've got all day. From this day forward I take more breaks and rest more often. Like I said, the first week was a learning curve. Lesson learned. Pace yourself and enjoy what you're doing. I sit on that bench for an entire hour. I'd been awake for more than 24 hours and I'm still wide awake.

After the sun has a chance to take the chill out of the air, I hit a gas station on the way out of town for a dookie-drop and refill of my water bottles. Although it was chilly last night, the forecast was calling for no clouds and temps hitting the high 90s. When the sun started climbing, it heated up with a vengeance. By 9 a.m. it's already in the low 90s and my bone chill is a lost dream I want to revisit. It's funny how we want what we can't have. Three days from now when we'd enter Missouri, I'd give anything for the high 90's.

Dave rings me up around 10 a.m. with the first "Where are you?" of the day.

"I have no idea," I tell him, "but I went through Phillipsburg a while ago."

He says he's coming up on Phillipsburg.

"You'll catch me soon so go up ahead about ten miles or so and wait. I'll need more water and snacks. And probably some shade."

He soon passes, flashers on so I know it's him. I give him the thumbs up and he jets on ahead. Bill pulls up shortly after and matches my pace. We chat a bit without slowing down. I tell him I'm good and that Dave just passed and is scouting a place to take a break in the next town. Bill hits the throttle and quickly catches Dave in the town of Smith Center.

I get the call 20 minutes later: "Take a left at the first road in town, follow it around a right bend, and we are in a park at a Farmer's Market."

By now I'm ready for a good long break. Like I said, I have all day and it isn't even noon yet.

Dave and Bill had made friends with some market vendors before I showed up. They'd explained what we were doing and why. I find the van and Harley parked under some shade trees in the town park that held the make-shift Saturday morning Farmers Market.

I pull up and Dave plops a small bag of cherry tomatoes in my hand. "These were free from Lois. I told her I don't like tomatoes, but you do. You should probably go say hi."

CHAPTER 12

Lois had a small card table that doubled as a vegetable stand. Her generous gesture moves me so deeply I immediately strip off every piece of non-essential clothing and head in her direction. I thank her for the tomatoes and we chat about my trip. She asks if she can pray for me. I say, "Absolutely." This was becoming a theme on the trip thus far. People wanting to pray for us. Gotta love Kansas.

People all over the world were praying for this trip, praying for my safety and the safety of the team. But people wanting to pray for me face to face and in real time was always an unexpected treat. A day hadn't gone by yet in Kansas where someone, somewhere didn't ask to pray for us.

It started the first night with the family that ran the Prairie Motel and Campground back in Anton, Colorado. We made a circle of 15 people or so in the middle of that cow pasture and they prayed for us. So by the time we found Lois, people praying for us was nothing new. It was the first time today though, but it wouldn't be the last.

We met some motorcyclists that afternoon at a gas station a few towns further along. They were talking to Bill about Harley's when I showed up. We made small talk about my trip and they wanted to pray for us. We prayed right then and there in that gas station parking lot and it was great. To me, you never turn down anyone that wants to pray for you. As far as I was concerned, I needed all the prayers I could get.

I'd been awake for more than 34 hours when we met those bikers, and I still had 15 miles to Mankato. The heat of the day was cranking up, so before I took off I dug out the cold-snap towel. This innovation is like some

NASA shit or something. It's a towel you dunk in luke-warm water, snap it, and it turns ice cold. This technology is way over my head, but whoever came up with it deserves the Nobel Prize. I also had a cold-snap vest Bill graciously bought me saying, "You're going to need this." And sure enough, during the next two 100 degree days the towel and vest were lifesavers. So with my snap towel around my neck, I crush the last 15 miles.

The Crest-Vue Motel is our stopping point today, the first hotel break we take. I'm going on five days without having changed anything but my underwear. I'm in dire need of a shower and change of clothes. My wife, Emily, called and said, "I've been watching your videos. Are you sponsored by Modelo or something? You haven't taken that shirt off yet." Hearing her voice always brings my anxiety down a bit.

Having a shower and a real bed is a treat. And now that Chef Bryce went home, we're stuck with a cooler full of Gatorade, V8, bananas, some yogurt, and floating bread and cheese.

I'm badly in need of a protein boost so we opt for the restaurant next door. It came highly recommended on the internet. ("It's the only restaurant within a hundred miles . . . but you know, it was excellent!") It's a steakhouse with an all-you-can-eat seafood buffet for $12.

Now, you must understand: Where I'm from, $12 will get you five peel and eat shrimp with a one oz. cocktail sauce . . . if you're lucky. But we are in Kansas and for 12 bucks we stuff ourselves silly. We eat smoked salmon, seafood salad, mahi mahi, prime rib, and bacon-wrapped filet mignon. No shit. I'm not making this up. It comes with an all-you-can-eat salad bar and the desert of your choice. Did I mention this is ALL you can eat?

We put a hurtin' on that place like Joey Chestnut at Coney Island on the 4th of July. It is all out gluttony, and I love every second of it. Two pounds of that all-you-can-eat shrimp that missed my mouth now clings to my Modelo shirt and it's time for my first shower in a week. Sorry Modelo shirt, finally to the dirty clothes bag you go. (Superstitious or not, I was not wearing that seafood-juice covered shirt tomorrow. By the way, Modelo, if you read this and want to sponsor my next trip, I'm all ears.)

After showers and patting our bellies (not each other's), Dave, Bill and I came up with a crazy idea to entertain ourselves that evening. Since we are constantly doing update videos for social media, we'd also been throwing around the idea of making some stupid videos, you know, throwback remakes of some of our favorite movie scenes. Bill and I love *Top Gun* and we'd already been quoting the movie to each other a little too much on the trip so far. So we decide to remake a scene from *Top Gun*. It involves dodging traffic on our little Kansas highway out front as well as several reshot interior scenes with Bill goofing around. It's good fun, pure silliness and it let out a lot of stress. It will take Dave three to four hours of editing just to get a minute long video, but that's his problem.

I've been awake just under 48 hours so I leave him to it and go to bed.

The forecast calls for 100 degrees tomorrow so as I drift off to sleep I'm already envisioning the inferno. I decide to call it '100 in 100.'

I'm not looking forward to the ride tomorrow.
At all.

CHAPTER 13

I would eventually cross the bridge into Marysville, Kansas, one hour before dusk, exhausted after nine hours on the bike. The weather report was correct. The temperature hit 102 degrees, a scorcher.

Limited access to shade takes its toll. Every ten miles or so I come upon a farm. The driveways are usually lined with trees and I stop at every one for a break from the merciless heat. The farm houses are usually set quite a ways back from the road so sitting under a tree for ten minutes couldn't be considered trespassing, could it? In the event I am discovered, I hope I can explain my situation. Worst case scenario I'd be shot on sight, best case scenario I'd be shot on sight. No more Ménière's. Just kidding . . . well . . . but no, really. Ok, jeez . . . best case scenario I'd be invited in for a cool glass of lemonade. And that sounds pretty good at this point. None of those things happen, however, and stopping often greatly slows my progress. But without the reprieve of shade I couldn't make my 100 miles.

On one occasion I'm cruising along—cold-snap vest on, yellow safety vest over that, and the cold-snap towel around my neck—and I pass a cornfield being irrigated. I pedal about 100 feet further and slam on the brakes. The metal contraption that irrigated the field in a giant circle reaches the road, and I thought it would feel so good to stand under that water. So I turn around and park my bike. 'This could work,' I think.

I trudge through brambles and thorns to get there, but my goal is single-minded: A fully-clothed shower in broad daylight. The corn won't mind, I decide. I walk down an infinite vegetation corridor as the long metal frame passes overhead. The misty water engulfs me, rewetting my cold-snap clothing, and soaking me to the bone.

It is glorious.

I only need 30 seconds then I scramble back, hop on my bike and say a silent "Thank you" to the farmer who might've saved my life. Ok, maybe that's an exaggeration, but those of you who live in central Kansas know what I mean. It's September for God's sake, and a complete scorcher.

The endless horizon shimmers with unreality and waves of heat. It begins playing tricks on my eyes as the road ahead looks hot and fuzzy, like smoke evaporating heaven-bound. This creates a mirage-like feeling, but I continue to pedal towards the blurry horizon.

I'm five miles from my destination when I look down and see I have no battery power. We'd already switched batteries twice that day and I still couldn't just glide into town free and clear.

Dammit.

One last battery change.

Bill had scouted a campsite for the night, a park right in the middle of Marysville with free camping. Yes, you heard that right. Free camping, right in the middle of the city.

Anyway, a quick call to Bill and Dave—"I can't make it. Yeah, five miles out"—and they hop in the van to meet me in the middle of the highway median, mere miles from my end point.

"This town is awesome," they tell me as we do the battery dance one more time. "The drive in is spectacular."

As they buzz off, it's not long before I see what they meant. The bridge into Marysville is a sight to behold. Truly the most beautiful landscape I've seen in days. I come to a river where American flags lining the bridge flap to the beat of the wind.

I take a right turn when I reach the middle of town and coast half a mile downhill. Soon an ordinary town park with swing sets, slides, basketball and tennis courts comes into view. Dave and Bill are lounging in a campsite right next to a swing set. Yes, it's an official campsite. Oh, and yeah, still hotter than hell out, but I'm thankful for what Bill found.

People are setting up tents on the grass as children have play dates with their friends. Mothers sit on benches chatting about their kids, the upcoming birthday party or the next PTA meeting. I think it's very unusual, yet spectacularly great, that the town of Marysville allowed this intermingling of families and campers just needing a place to rest for the night.

Marysville is the biggest town we've seen since Denver. With a population of just over 4,000 it feels like arriving in New York City or Chicago. It's even big enough to have a Walmart! I immediately love the feel of the place and it quickly becomes my favorite campsite so far.

We relax in the shade of the giant trees and watch a large black squirrel comfortably straddle the crossbar of the swing set staring at us with intense interest. Bill and I lounge in camp chairs and enjoy a cold Modelo. Dave sits on the cooler and updates the social media. I'm more relaxed than I have been in awhile. But it's still in the high 90s at 10 p.m.

It's not long before I sack out and catch up on social media, then turn on a ball game. I leave the rain cover off my tent, and with just the brown mosquito mesh between me and the sky, I sleep like a baby.

I accomplished my goal today: 96 1/2 miles in 102 degree heat, '100 in 100.' Fuck you, Ménière's. I got you again! You lose, I win. I was feeling pretty good, but what I didn't know as I drifted off was that tomorrow I'd be fighting for my life.

I would visit the ENT three times throughout the next year. My first vertigo attack came after my second visit. My doctor hadn't done dick for me so far, but I called him for a third appointment anyway. I told him I'd become dizzy and nauseous the week before. I was vomiting and couldn't stand up. He told me I'd had a vertigo attack. I'd never heard of a vertigo attack.

I liked the movie 'Vertigo' with Jimmy Stewart, however, and thought 'vertigo' was basically limited to a fear of heights or some shit like that. I liked the word 'vertigo' and thought it'd make a great name for a band. "You wanted the best, you got the best! Get ready, Cleveland, the best band in the land . . . VERTIGO!" Flash pots burst and cannons roar on the first note . . .

But now I no longer think it's cool.

When I say the word 'vertigo,' I spit it out like spoiled milk.

My ENT then informed me there was a possibility I had Ménière's Disease.

#1-What the fuck is Ménière's Disease?

#2-There's no way in hell I have a 'disease.' Yes, my ear rings and I fell down last week and couldn't get back up. But a disease? . . . I don't think so. I'm healthy, athletic, I'm a musician, and I go to work every day and work my ass off to provide for my family.

I have a 'disease?'

I can't accept that.

The doc said there was no test for it so he couldn't say for sure. It could also be a brain tumor. My eyes glaze over. A fucking WHAT? Now I have a brain tumor? This is spiraling way out of control. And fast.

He leaned back in his chair and put a hand on his chin—so cliche for a doctor. "It might also be an autoimmune deficiency, or a loose bone chip in your left ear . . . or a thyroid issue." I slumped in my chair and stared at a poster on the wall depicting the workings of the inner ear. This is preposterous! . . . Silly talk! . . . A cruel joke!

Eight years later I tell you the truth, this is no fucking joke.

PART 4

Missouri: When it rains, it pours!

Marysville, Kansas-St. Joseph, Missouri, 100 miles
(didn't make it)
Marysville, Kansas-Hiawatha, Kansas, 60 miles
(barely made it)
Hiawatha, Kansas-Cameron, Missouri, 100 miles
Cameron, Missouri-Brookfield, Missouri, 65 miles
Brookfield, Missouri-Hannibal, Missouri, 123 miles

CHAPTER 14

Day 8

Why do I have to ride 100 miles a day? I've been asked this question many times since the beginning of my trip. There were several reasons for my thought process: Riding five miles a day was easy, so I wanted to push myself beyond my comfort level. Next, we only had a month to complete the trip. Why a month? We set the boundaries, after all.

This is the deal: A week long trip would've been far too short to be interesting on social media. A five-month trip would've been far too long and would drag-out too much for social media. Besides, we didn't have the travel budget to do something so extreme.

The most important reason was that when I hit the border of Missouri, I wanted to be ahead of schedule. As far ahead of schedule as I could be. It would take all the pressure off if I needed more rest days, or if there were days when I couldn't do 100 miles. Being ahead of schedule gave me a mental and physical buffer. And on top of that, I wanted to push myself beyond what I thought I could handle. Only then would I learn more about my disease and how to live with it.

I wanted answers. I wanted to walk away from the trip with a new understanding of who I was.

When we left Marysville, Kansas, the plan was to do roughly 100 miles to St. Joseph, Missouri. I booked a night in a hotel there for showers, a real bed and a rest day. But Mother Nature and my illness had other plans. The first red flag was that although I'd had a good night last night, in the morning I sat up, and immediately knew: Uh, oh. Today was going to be a fight.

Yes, I'd slept well last night, but after I tore down my tent and drank my obligatory V8 and Gatorade I felt a little off. I felt shaky, dizzier than usual, and my brain was foggy and unfocused. More often than not this is my daily existence. I've had some speed bumps thrown at me so far, namely my emotional breakdown on day three along with micro-managing the team and driving them crazy with my incessant chatter and irritability, impossible levels of anxiety, and an attitude of constant catastrophic doom.

And those were my *good* days.

Within the Ménière's community we never say, "Have a good day." It's always, "I hope you have more good days than bad." And truth be told, there really are no good days. There may be days where I don't fight my symptoms as much, but hell, it's still a constant battle for survival.

The point of my ride is to battle, so lying in bed today isn't an option. And at the moment I throw my tent into the van in the middle of a city park in Marysville, Kansas, I am far from my bed.

91

Far, far from my bed.

But the thought of a hotel room that night brightens my mood if ever so slightly. A hot shower, clean clothes, and hopefully a playoff hockey game if I was lucky. Yes, this was 2020, the year of COVID, and hockey was playing in September. Anyway, feeling good, bad or ugly, I'm off to the city of St. Joseph, Missouri, roughly 100 miles away.

When I finally leave the park at 8 a.m., it's already in the low 90s. I think, 'Shit, by noon it will be over 100 degrees.' Marysville quickly falls behind in my rearview mirror and once again I'm surrounded by corn and soybeans. The wind soon picks up to a fierce surge and hits me square in the face. I lean into it with little enthusiasm, and start to cry.

Crying is a release when my symptoms become overwhelming. It's like opening a pressure-release valve on an air tank that's too full. Crying is something I can't control and stopped trying to control long ago. It's my brain's way of saying, "Hey, I've had enough. I'm full. And managing today will take all the energy I've got, so you need to cry a little to get back to feeling somewhat normal." That day out of Marysville I would cry a lot for the first four hours. The wind was relentless and didn't alleviate the heat in the least. There wasn't a cloud in the sky, or a tree to sit under, in sight.

I glance down and notice my battery is draining quickly. I was working the bike hard and I imagined it felt like me, completely one-hundred percent exhausted. I call the guys and alert them to my dilemma. I wouldn't be able to make 20 miles on this battery. When we eventually switch that battery out, the next one drains a mere 25 miles later. Well, shit. My attitude was teetering between frustration and full-on nuclear meltdown.

I ride into the tiny hamlet of Seneca, Kansas. I quickly find Bill at a gas station and I know Dave has been in town for some time, desperately seeking a grounded outlet to charge the battery faster than the van could. Turns out Dave has found an outlet near the press box of a nearby high school baseball stadium and was siphoning electrons while trying not to be spotted by nearby soccer parents.

Dave was also a bit frayed that day because he is backed up on social media postings from not having internet service to his phone or laptop for the past few days while we were in the middle of BFE Kansas. From the gas station I call Dave to ask where he is and he tells me, "Turn around." I turn and see that the baseball stadium is about two hundred yards directly behind me.

"Is the battery almost done?" I ask in desperation.

"Not even close." Dave informs me.

Shit.

I've barely gone 50 miles and it's already past noon. I've had a NASA sized wind tunnel smashing me in my face all day, we are already on battery change number two, and then Dave reports that the battery I need wasn't anywhere near ready?

For the first time we have two empty batteries at the same time. Dammit! I slouch against the shaded side of the gas station, completely wiped out and stalled out. I can barely see through the sunglasses I'm wearing so I ask Bill if he could help me find something to clean them. He finds a napkin and I hand him the glasses.

"What's this white shit all over them?" he asks innocently.

"I'm not sure. It's probably salt," I reply.

"How'd you get salt all over them?" he quips.

"Because I've been crying for the past four hours," I say ashamedly.

Dave had since brought the battery to the gas station and we plug it in at the wall where we sit. It's charging slower than Mother Teresa trying to climb the Empire State Building.

'This is going to take six to eight hours!' I fume to myself.

Dammit!

We each sit staring straight ahead, tired and frustrated as the sun rolls by overhead like its ass is on fire. The day is moving entirely too quick for me.

I am pissed.

The three of us discuss what it would look like to go another 25 miles, sit for another six hours to charge a battery, then do it all over again. By my calculation that would put me arriving at the hotel in St. Joseph around 4 a.m. That was not acceptable and I sink further into frustration.

We begin to discuss alternative strategies when someone says, "Why don't we put the most charged battery in now, and you can get going for what it's worth. We can plug the other one in here and charge it for a while then leap frog you and see where we're at."

Agreed.

We switch the battery out and I take off, Bill and Dave remaining on the shady side of the gas station shooting the shit while Blackie charges.

Out on the road I'm quickly at my breaking point (if I wasn't already there miles ago) and decide to call my wife. I need to hear her voice and calm myself down. I hadn't come up short on miles yet and I didn't know what to do. I tell her the situation and without pause, she says, "Why not just get as far as you can on that battery, have Dave pick you up there, drive to the hotel, then go back to the exact same spot in the morning?"

Brilliant!

I immediately calm down. This plan makes sense. God, I love that woman.

Really I should have seen it myself, but this day is kicking my ass and I'm far from thinking straight. At least I was done crying like a little baby. Dave and Bill soon catch up to me and I tell them the plan. They seem relieved to see me calm and somewhat upbeat.

Bill shoots on ahead to check us into the hotel in St. Joseph and Dave is staying close to see where I'll land, but also because I'm struggling mightily. I get as far as Hiawatha, Kansas, and Dave stops to give me the other battery. I tell him, "No need, I'm done, I can't do this anymore today. Let's get the hell out of here." We toss the bike in the van and head for Missouri.

The final tally on the day was 60 miles.

Our plan now was to backtrack 40 miles the next day to Hiawatha to make up the ground. But I call my sister, Karen, and tell her what happened and she offers to pay for a second night in the hotel so we can have a full day off tomorrow. Fantastic. Now we can sleep in, get some much needed rest and take care of some odds and ends that've gone wanting. In two days we will backtrack to Hiawatha where I stopped and start my 100 mile day from there.

95

We get to the hotel and Bill joins us in the lobby. "Boys, we're in Missouri," he says. But we'd already been quite welcomed to Missouri. How? Well, I'll tell you.

It seemed customary for each and every person with a car to rev their engine into a full-on Top Fuel Dragster burnout at every stoplight. This happened several times as we pulled up to the hotel. Did this happen in Kansas? Not at all. We were uniquely in Missouri. And I thought, 'I wish to hell I owned a tire store in this town.'

We check into our room and find we are able to time the stoplight outside our window by the roar of the Top Fuel Dragster contest every time red turns green. I mean, I'm someone who's lost most of the hearing in my left ear, and my right ear sucks too, but this shit was even too much for me. Maybe it was just the part of town we were in or a cultural moment that was happening, but this went on everywhere we went in the state. It was hilarious, entertaining, and a bit disturbing all at the same time.

The most amusing display of this sham-foolery happens that night after dinner. The three of us walk around the corner to grab a bite to eat and afterwards Dave goes straight back to the hotel to edit videos and do his thing.

Bill and I, wanting to stretch our legs a bit, circle the block in search of more Modelo. We find a shop and buy a 12-pack and figure we can shortcut behind a shopping mall to get back to the hotel. We cut down a gravel alley that opens to the back of said shopping mall, which because of the pandemic, is completely shuttered.

It's dusk and no one is around. But to our surprise, well, not really, there's a small, beat up Chevy S10 ripping donuts in the empty parking lot on straight up bare pavement. I mean, sure, we used to do donuts in iced-over parking lots in high school, but this was bare-assed straight-up dry asphalt.

Crazy!

Anyway, I'm thinking this must be some bored high school kids doing what bored high school kids do. I did it in high school, now they're doing it. Bill and I admire the tenacity of this ongoing display with awe, reverence, and gut-busting amusement. Five minutes later the Dukes of Hazzard stop. A cloud of smoke that engulfed the vehicle dissipates and disappears as if by magic. The driver's door opens and a lady that had to be in her upper 60's steps out. Her old man, beer belly and all, gets out of the passenger side. And, of course, he's not wearing a shirt. Together they walk to the front of the truck, rest their hind asses against the front bumper and fire up a smoke. Apparently doing a donut on bare pavement was tantamount to great sex in Missouri.

Who knew?

Bill and I look at each other and completely fall out laughing. What the fuck planet have we landed on all of a sudden? We are, and sorry for the cliche, DEFINITELY not in Kansas anymore.

Back at the room, we put our beer in the mini fridge to the vroom-screech of 'Look at my badass pickup truck!' glory as the stoplight once again changes outside our window. What can I say, Missouri? You're something.

I'm completely wiped out, so we take the next day to rest. Bill and I watch movies, Dave is editing videos for social media, and we discuss my route from Hiawatha, Kansas, through St. Joseph, Missouri, and on to Cameron, Missouri, our stopping point the next day.

Getting through St. Joseph on my bike was going to

be the biggest logistical test of the trip so far. Up till then we hadn't had to deal with any heavy traffic issues because we'd only been in very rural areas of Colorado and Kansas. The largest town, Marysville, Kansas, was still incredibly small by any relative metric. St. Joseph, on the other hand, was a fairly large city and there was only one way into the city—the Pony Express Bridge. It was just like any other city bridge over a large river, but everything in that part of the country was named in one way or another for the Pony Express. And once you crossed it (assuming I lived), there was barely a shoulder, with on-ramps and exit ramps going in a million different directions like Dr. Seuss' Hoober-Bloob Highway.

It was madness.

And on top of that, once I got across the bridge (assuming I lived) I wasn't even sure which exit ramp I needed since all the ramps looked the same, weren't marked very well, and it all looked like a Medusa head of spaghetti once you got into the middle of it.

On top of THAT, if I failed to hit the correct exit right after the bridge, the shoulder literally reduced to *nothing* and the speed limit was 75 mph with all manner of cars, SUVs, pickup trucks and semis hauling balls. (Not literally hauling balls, I mean going fast. Well, unless it was a truck carrying sporting goods, then it might've literally been hauling balls).

So on our rest day, Bill, Dave, and I have many discussions about how best to get me through the madness of St. Joseph highways alive, which even includes Bill possibly doing a few scouting runs on his motorcycle to pick a route most likely to keep me from getting splattered. But somehow that idea gets lost in the shuffle of the day, and there's no test run completed. For the first time on the trip, we face the imminent possibility that I might not live through the next day. Yeah, I mean it. This is heavy. And we all feel it.

I fitfully sleep unaware the temperature outside is taking a record nose dive. It was over 100 degrees yesterday, but by morning it will be 43 degrees and raining. Raining! We hadn't seen a drop of water from the sky so far, and now not only rain but cold.

I was mentally unprepared.

As I've mentioned, I never really sleep well at night, so no matter what time I go to bed I'm usually up around 4 or 5 a.m preparing to leave hours before the rest of the team enters REM sleep.

Usually Dave and/or Bill come to life the moment, or close to it, when I'm rolling out of camp to hit the road. Dave, being a dyed-in-the-wool night owl, had been trying to get to bed early each night to be ready for my early morning take offs. But it wasn't working out for him. He was not getting much sleep because our schedule was not in his wheelhouse. But he was doing his best to keep up with my hours, dictated not so much by what I'd ideally want but by the Monster of Ménière's.

As Dave pulls the covers over his head at 9:30 p.m., I tell him I'm setting the alarm for the butt crack of dawn. "That's fine," he says resignedly, and I turn on a hockey game. I know I'll be up for a while. Turns out I barely slept at all.

The plan was that Dave would take me back to Hiawatha, then he'd drive to the hotel to meet Bill. I'd show up eventually, we'd do a battery switch, then I'd continue on to Cameron. That is, if I made *the bridge* and what came after it.

Precisely at 6:30 in the a.m. I roll my bike out of the hotel as quietly as possible, Dave in tow. We step outside, and BAM, it's freezing cold with a hard drizzle. Oh man, I'm thinking, rain and cold? Haven't had to deal with either so far. And the bridge . . . and the traffic? Shit. At least we're so early the traffic should be minimal across the bridge. That was one thing insomnia had going for it.

By the time we hit Hiawatha, it's fifty degrees and raining hard. Standing by the side of the road I gear up with extra layers, including black long johns over my gel shorts. I add a long sleeve shirt over my KISS concert shirt. This was given to me before the trip by my good friend, Chuck. He's the biggest KISS fan in the world and it's a great old school shout out to Metalheads everywhere. I yank on my blue pullover hoodie, and a rain jacket over that. I slip into my safety vest with a winter hat and warm gloves. The ensemble is complete. Oh, yeah, one more thing: I also tie a red bandana around my face like a spaghetti western bandit preparing to rob a bank. It will keep my face warm, but the downfall is my glasses fog up, so I decide to tuck them into my ass bag and ride without them to start.

We unload my bike into the freezing, driving rain and I ask Dave to shoot a quick video. He shields himself against the van wrapped in full winter coat and hat while I stand taking the brunt of Mother Nature like Jim Cantore on hurricane duty with the Weather Channel. Dave looks relieved to hop in the warm, dry van and as he speeds away I'm a little envious. But I turn to the Monster within and say, "Let's do this, asshole!" and off I go.

As I said, with a population of 80,000, St. Joseph is an actual city. The rain mercifully let up and turned to a light drizzle as I crossed the bridge, found my exit ramp, and cruised into the business district with little problem.

Starting early was definitely the right choice. With traffic so thin it was easy to read the signs and I could even stop and look around to get my bearings if it came to that. The hustle and bustle of crossing the bridge in late afternoon two days prior was nearly nonexistent. As I turn north toward downtown St. Joseph, I ease my pace and enjoy riding in an urban environment for the first time since we left Denver.

Dave:

Today's culture of texting and phoning while driving, compounded with the unpredictability of Steve's Ménière's, gave rise to a legitimate amount of worry that at some point in this trip, a truck or car would simply wipe him off the road—game over.

That was a constant drumbeat of tension that underwrote the whole trip whenever he was on the road. Being the number one person in charge of seeing that he lived through each day, the very real possibility of this was never far from my mind. And here was the first big test, getting his ass through St. Joseph alive.

It was no joke.

The first time we drove through St. Joe in mid-afternoon I saw the traffic and the roads and thought, 'Oh, my God. How's he going to do this? . . . On a bike?' The fact that riding a bike on an interstate highway was totally illegal was an issue, but more problematic was that, assuming he lived coming over the bridge, if he didn't hit his exit exactly right he'd be immediately thrust into a crazy-fast, busy highway with absolutely no shoulder.

None at all.

It was simply the lane then concrete wall. And if he got caught in that, it'd spell certain doom. So spending a day discussing how to best navigate all that was a big deal.

We even talked about him possibly rolling his bike across a railroad bridge just north of the highway bridge, since that was the only other route across the river at all.

That would put him straight into downtown St. Joe and eliminate the whole traffic and truck danger altogether. But looking on the map, there was no easy way to get him onto the railroad bridge, and besides, would he have room if a train happened along? Steve pretty much dismissed it outright. "How would I ride my bike on train tracks anyway?" I guess he had a point.

Pushing the bike across the tracks seemed reasonable to me, but he thought it'd take too much time.

"I'll just deal with traffic," he concluded and that's pretty much where we left it, aside from discussing whether Bill should take a test run on his Harley to make sure the route we picked was viable.

Our chosen route would take Steve across the bridge, then up north through downtown, east past our hotel, then straight out of town on his way to Cameron. A 70 mile day, cold, wet and rainy, but hopefully doable.

When I dropped Steve off at the starting point in Hiawatha, I hope it's now understandable that the thought, 'This might actually be the last time I ever see him,' was a real one. The possible danger of this trip was now very real and in both our faces as we stood beside the highway that morning and took the video.

When he stopped speaking, I stepped into the windy rain, hugged him and said my usual, "Good luck." What else could I say? It's not everyday you leave someone you care about and think, 'This might actually be the last time I see them alive.' But this was that time.

And it wasn't easy.

When I finally approach the bridge, I know this is the moment of truth. I figure the guys back at the hotel were nervous, and so was I. I had to hit my exit, I could not miss it. Even this early without much traffic, if I missed the exit right after the bridge I'd be in trouble. I crossed the river and was concentrating so hard my hand grips were complaining, '*Damn boy, quit squeezing so hard!*' I see the word 'North' on a sign and take it. I'm not sure this is correct, but I know I need to go north. Turns out I was right. Whew!

Now I am on city streets and feel at home. I love cities. I slow down to get my bearings and enjoy the scenery. I pass the courthouse and old warehouses closed up decades ago. I'm firmly enmeshed in the Rust Belt, and this will continue for the next three states. The road takes a lazy right as I pass homeless people and boarded-up storefronts. I am headed east again and will make a quick stop at the hotel for a battery change before taking off for Cameron, Missouri.

At one point, I'm waiting at a stoplight and a cop pulls up next to me. He looks over with his best Dirty Harry smirk and gives me a nod with his chin. There's only a slight drizzle, but for the past three hours I was in a freezing downpour. I am soaked to the bone and probably look like a fish out of water, literally. I nod my chin back, and he speeds away in search of greater trouble.

I stop at our hotel to change clothes and tell the guys I made it OK. I get a fully charged battery and navigate my way back to Route 36, which has now become a two lane divided highway with very heavy traffic. And the rain picked up again, too. Route 36 through Kansas was a ghost town for the most part, but the same Route 36 through Missouri might as well be Interstate 70, a major highway across America that doesn't allow bicycles because of safety concerns.

Social media comments on our videos around this time brought forth "What happened? Are you guys on I-70 now?" and "Man, that looks super dangerous with all those trucks." And they were right . . . well, except for the I-70 part. Nope, we were still tooling along on 36, and yeah, it would've sucked ass with the traffic and no rain, but traffic and rain . . . and cold. It sucked!

If I caught a glimpse of an approaching truck in my rearview mirror, I'd get ready to brace myself. I'd have to grab on tight as the wind rocked me side to side. Add in the rain, and every truck that flew past also slammed me in the back with a bucket of water.

Normal trucks were bad enough, but the trucks that affected me most were the hog trucks. Pretty much rolling jail cells for pigs, these trucks were steel cages on wheels with tiny slots for the bacon to breathe.

On a normal day through Kansas they'd drive by and I'd get a blast of pig shit smell. Uncomfortable, yes, but no big deal. In a downpour it was a whole new ballgame. I was pacing at 18 mph but those rolling pigsties were going 75 plus. It took everything I had to concentrate on simply staying on the shoulder, much less avoiding the random car parts, bags of trash, rocks and glass that cluttered my narrow lane.

When I'd catch that glimpse of a truck in my rearview mirror, I'd brace myself, soaked to the core, and start pleading, 'Don't be a pig truck . . . Don't be a pig truck . . . ' I'd chant this mantra over and over in my head. And 'Whoosh!' Rain mixed with road-scum mixed with pig-pee, pig-shit, and pig-saliva would wash over my entire body, and often into my mouth, as I rocked side to side in the wind trying to hold the shoulder.

Miserable.

Fucking miserable.

And my back covered in pigshit was a smell that never really went away. On top of all this, I was pretty much going on 48 hours again with no sleep. Last night's insomnia/anxiety about making it through St. Joe alive was catching up with a vengeance.

I need a distraction, so I call my dad. It'd become a habit that when I was struggling to stay focused I'd pull down my headset mic and call my mother or father. We'd talk about sports, weather, my destination for the day, anything and everything . . . whatever.

My father's kitchen in Ohio had even become an ad hoc command center. Maps and charts apparently covered his table so when I called him he could relay information about the approaching towns. He would tell me the population, the important community information, where I could shop for supplies or places to stay.

Today after being pigshit-ed for hours and the MD Monster fighting me like hell, I ring him up.

"I'm struggling today, Pop, it's a tough one," I tell him.

He asks how many more miles till I stop.

"The boys are five miles ahead in Cameron," I replied.

I hear papers flip and maps unfold. His wife, Carol, is in the background asking, "Where is he, where is he?"

Dave had called me earlier and said, "After you go under a highway overpass we are the next exit on the right."

I navigate the next rise and see the overpass. "Hey Pop, I think I'm within a couple miles of the guys."

He says he's happy to stay on the line as long as it takes to get me where I'm going.

The next thing I know my bike starts to wobble. I look down. "Damn it Pop, my front tire is going flat. Got to call Dave, thanks for talking."

Dave drives back and picks me up; we throw the bike in the van and meet with Bill to fix the tire. "I'm fucking over it today," I tell Bill. This was the hardest day yet and I was done.

Dave works on social media as Bill and I are fixing my flat tire. We discover that I picked up a thorn in my front tire days ago and it's finally worked its way through to poke the inner tube.

We cracked on Dave earlier for blowing two tires at the same time on his bike with thorns at a park in the middle of Kansas. Now I feel a little guilty for bashing him since I must've picked up a thorn at the exact same place, it just took longer to penetrate my thick tires. I was riding on 60 PSI mountain bike tires. Dave had paper thin street tires. We replaced my inner tube and put on a new tread. I pump the tire with a small, handheld pump.

Bill tells me to ride around a bit because he wasn't certain the bead was set. I ride in a circle for 20 seconds in the motel parking lot and say it feels fine. But rolling in a circle at 5 mph is a far cry from doing 20 mph for an eight hour day. I should've been more focused because it'd soon come back to bite me.

We all go to bed that night beat down and exhausted . . . the team normally so, and me, about a million times worse than the 'normal' person. Little do I know, as I drift toward exhausted sleep, tomorrow will be worse.

CHAPTER 16

I wake up feeling like shit. The rain picked up again after St. Joseph yesterday and now Missouri is covered by one gigantic rain storm. It'd be that way for the next three days, the entire time we were in the state.

Thanks for nothing, Missouri.

The barometric pressure drops when rain storms move in, which is just another Ménière's sucker-punch to me. Imagine sticking a Q-tip in your ear so far it causes a sharp pain. But this sharp pain is consistent and it can't be alleviated. That's the pressure that fills my ears when rain moves in. It also gives me the pleasure of a mild headache. Great . . . Not a sharp pain, but a dull throbbing behind my eyes. It's fucking annoying and debilitating.

With my head in the Monster's vice-like grip I decide to see what I can accomplish today.

It turns out, not much.

I physically feel so horrible I send Dave out alone to do our morning video. We'd gotten in the routine of doing a morning and evening video for the people following our trip. I push back the curtain in the room and see Dave standing in the middle of a field in the rain talking into his phone/camera . . . with sunglasses on. He shows me the video when he comes back in and at the end of it he says, "And I'm wearing sunglasses for no reason. Peace out!" Funny. I like the touch and need all the lightheartedness I can get.

Brookfield, Missouri, is our target destination today—at 100 miles.

Great . . .

Adding to my ear pain and dull headache are the other ever-present symptoms: dizziness, nausea, brain fog, lack of concentration and balance issues. I can barely stand up. This is the first day I really question what I'm doing out here.

The biggest issue I have with my chronic illness is that it's not terminal. This means it's NOT going to kill me. But 'chronic' means it's ever-present and I will live like this until the day I die. These are days I wish I had an expiration date. I know it sounds cruel and I'm not suicidal. I'm just tired of this shit.

I had two good friends die of cancer this year. One last spring and the other two days before I left Denver. They were my age. I saw what they went through and the fight they put up to survive. I saw what it did to their families and loved ones. I don't mean to sound flip, but today I was jealous. I really wished I could just be done. But as the subtitle to this book suggests, if I can't be done (yet), then hopefully I can find a way to make a difference. Love and respect from my friends who passed away definitely kept me in the fight out there in the middle of miserable Missouri, and I was sure they were rooting me on. (Love you, Raelynn and Sue.)

I love my life, but more than that I love my wife and son. I don't really want to die, but at the same time I want to stop suffering. It's a difficult conundrum to live with every day. Today is just one of those days I want to curl up and disappear. But the show must go on ...

I layer myself in the previous day's rain-gear and we set out once again. The cold and rain hits me like a 2 x 4 (as if I needed that on top of everything else I had to deal with) and the guys look at me like I'm some crazed, Tim Burton-esque skeleton. With dark clouds of doom hanging overhead and the MD Monster unrelentingly squeezing my brain, we leave Cameron, Missouri, en route to Brookfield, Missouri.

God help us all.

CHAPTER 17

This was, by far, the most miserable day of my trip.

One mile in and I'm soaking wet and cold. On top of the earache, headache, and all my other symptoms going ape shit, I realized Bill was right; my tire bead is not set. This means I have an air bubble in my tire. The tire is not 'pure.' A fully inflated tire would be balanced and round. My tire is far from that. Every rotation goes thump, thump, thump. Although the shoulder is flat and smooth, I feel like I'm riding down railroad tracks. Total rookie mistake on my part.

Soaking wet, in the pouring rain, I squint without glasses into a monster headwind trying my damndest to keep my bike under me. I'd give my left nut for 100 degrees in Kansas right now. Ten miles in I am completely miserable. The pig trucks I dealt with yesterday haven't let up one bit, so that funhouse of horror keeps slopping me in the back with buckets of pig shit, over and over. Fuck.

I pull over and book us rooms at the Martin House Motel in Brookfield, Missouri. I'm going to need a hot shower and a bed tonight, that's for sure. The Martin House was right off Route 36 and the pictures online look nice. I thought $45 a night was a bargain for such a luxurious looking place. It ended up being far from the Waldorf-Astoria.

But I'm just trying to survive the day's ride and need a warm, dry place to look forward to. Someplace I could escape the constant Ca-thump, Ca-thump, Ca-thump of my front tire, which is driving me insane beyond words. I'm exhausted, freezing cold and—Ca-thump, Ca-thump, Ca-thump—can't think of one good reason to keep pedaling. Well, there was one, and it was the people that were depending on me and watching my trip around the world.

A heated discussion begins in my head: Our GoFundMe account continued to climb and we were picking up new followers on social media daily. We raised more than $7,000 so far, $6,500 more than I expected.

Between the large sums of money being raised and our social media sites gaining momentum, I felt a responsibility not to fail. I felt like I was under a worldwide microscope, so I kept pedaling. I told myself, 'Isn't this why you're out here doing this? To bring attention and awareness to the disability and chronic illness you suffer?'

At 25 miles I tell myself, 'Just go one more mile' Ca-thump, Ca-thump, Ca-thump. At 26 miles I say: 'Just go one more mile . . . ' Ca-thump, Ca-thump, Ca-thump. I repeat this until mile 30. I argue inside my head, 'You're an idiot. You can't keep going.' Ca-thump, Ca-thump, Ca-thump.

'But people are watching.'

'But you're freezing, you're an idiot.'

'Yeah, but people are supporting me and are rooting for me.' Ca-thump, Ca-thump, Ca-thump.

'You're still an idiot and you're miserable.'

'But I can't stop now. I backtracked once already, I can't do it again.' Ca-thump, Ca-thump, Ca-thump.

WTF? I am driving myself insane and so is my tire. Aaaaaaaargh!

For the next five miles I fight to pedal, my teeth are chattering, and I can't feel my knee caps. I was wearing fingerless gloves to change gears easily, and when I look down the argument inside my head slams to a halt. My fingers have turned purple. I call Dave in complete disgust, but with a tinge of relief. "Come and get me. I think I'm going hypothermic."

In the meantime Bill has buzzed ahead and

checked us into the motel we would affectionately nickname 'Shawshank.' The Martin House Motel was basically a painted cinder block. The layout was crazy, as if it were once a long, concrete warehouse that formerly housed a chicken operation or something. But after Dave retrieved me on the highway, cold, drenched and defeated, I didn't care one way or another. To me it was like pulling up to the Four Seasons.

Bill and I share a room and Dave has his own. He still has work to do and needs space that is quiet. Bill and I, on the other hand, are always carrying on, cracking each other up, and/or cracking on each other. We drink beer like we're in a frat house and we never shut up.

I enter our room, strip down to my skin and hang my wet clothing all over the room to dry. Then I collapse onto my bed. There is no way around it. Today sucked ass. The weather and the beast got the best of me and I just want to forget it ever happened. So far Missouri was a far cry from the sunshine and cornfields of Kansas, and I wasn't sure I could do this anymore.

I needed another day off, so we booked the same rooms for the next night, but I knew whenever we started again I'd have to backtrack the 30 miles I fell short today. And the thought of that turned my stomach.

After a few hours resting on the bed, I climb down from my ledge of despair and we walk three blocks in a light drizzle to a quaint little Mexican restaurant. The restaurant is cozy and the decor is bright and uplifting. As we eat, we discuss making another movie spoof. We decide a scene from *Planes, Trains and Automobiles* would be our next venture and we laugh our asses off discussing what we could do.

As we return to Shawshank, I have pretty much gotten over the misfortunes of the day and we rehearse and film the Steve Martin/John Candy "Two Pillows" scene from *P, T and A*. Dave heads to his room to edit, and Bill and I watch the nightly playoff hockey game. Then it's lights out and we live to fight another day.

CHAPTER 18

The next morning we awake to more rain. We debate briefly whether I'd go make up the miles from yesterday right now, or rest the whole day and just do it tomorrow.

Bill and Dave look at me: "Really it comes down to how you're feeling. Do you want to do it today or rest?"

I step outside. The entire state seems fogged in, the rain a soft drizzle and the temp was clammy but not freezing. "I'll go today."

But the first order of business is to fix the issues with my front tire. I couldn't take another day of Ca-thump, Ca-thump, Ca-thump. Bill and I turn the bike upside down right in the middle of our motel room and let out air, only to pump it up again. We spin the tire and there it is, still. The small bubble that caused the 'Ca-thump.' We look at each other, stumped. What's going on here?

I look at Dave: "Can you get Bryce on the phone?"

Bryce was our master mechanic for the trip. Before he'd left us in the middle of Kansas he said we could call him anytime for any and all things mechanical. We were grateful for that. We ring him up.

He says, "Seems the tire's not getting enough air. What're you using?"

We tell him we have a hand-pump that basically quits right before hitting the desired PSI. We didn't think it mattered.

"Do you have anything stronger?"

We look at each other. We did. In the van, we had an electric pump Dave and I's Aunt Stephanie insisted we take along on the trip. Turns out, it was sage advice.

We hang up with Bryce, take the bike outside in the drizzle (the pump is a cigarette lighter adapter only) and hook everything up. We pre-program it for 60 PSI and let 'er rip. It quickly closes in on 50 psi and the tire is hard as a rock. I say, "That's enough."

But Bill and Dave in unison say, "No, it's not. Wait for it."

'Wait for what?' I'm thinking. 'For the whole damn thing to blow up in my face?' I turn and see Dave slowly backing away from the van. 'I gotta override them,' I think, reaching to unplug it at the exact moment there's a small pop.

"There it is," Bill says with pride and relief. The tire is fixed. The bead has set perfectly.

"Who knew?" someone says out loud, I don't know who, but we look at each other and silently thank our trusty absentee bike mechanic who once again came through in a pinch.

Bill hops in the back of the van with the bike. I climb into the passenger seat, already dressed and ready to go. Dave fires up the van and we backtrack 30 miles. We make a video for social media as we're driving, then I'm back on the road.

I cover the miles in no time and join Bill for breakfast at the local greasy spoon while Dave bikes around town for a bit of exercise. Resident waitresses Opal and Jennifer treat Bill and me like royalty. They find our trip intriguing and donate some of their tips to our ride. This is humbling to say the least.

I have yet to get over the generosity and open-heartedness of people across the Midwest. It will definitely be the people, not the weather or the geography, that is most memorable about this trip. On the way out the door, we take some pictures with Opal and Jennifer for social media (always with permission), and now it's time to rest.

Bill was only supposed to be with us for the first week. To the delight of Dave and I, a week ago Bill called and requested another week off work to continue on the trip. He made the call when we were in St. Joseph; this would carry him all the way through Missouri. It's been two weeks and Bill will leave first thing in the morning and ride 740 miles straight home.

Come evening we decide to make another 80s movie skit for social media. We decide on the Grace/Ed Rooney office scene from *Ferris Bueller's Day Off* and crack each other up again with another 'Ménière's: On the VertiGO' classic.

This day might have been the most problem free of the trip so far, but when we get ready to hit the sack, the air is heavy with the weight of knowing Bill is leaving us in the morning. Bill will be missed. His humor and relaxed personality has been a great equalizer for me and Dave's ying/yang demeanor.

In the morning Bill and I stand in the cold, fog, and drizzle infested parking lot of Shawshank and make our farewell video. I thank him for being with us, we hug, then Dave films Bill on his Harley and I on my bike as we ride off side by side. But when we get to the highway, for the first time in two weeks, Bill heads west as I turn east.

Godspeed, my friend. You have no idea how much you've meant to this trip.

Out on Route 36 the weather has cleared and it's a lot nicer by mid-morning. The forecast looks great for the next ten days and this lifts my spirits. My symptoms have subsided somewhat, but the days of rain have taken their toll. To finish this trip, I was going to have to dig deep.

Dave and I being on our own for the first time is an odd feeling. Team 'On the VertiGO' is now down to two. Our destination for today is Quincy, Missouri, on the Illinois border. Dave calls me sometime during the morning with great news. Our youngest brother Brian and his son Emmitt have driven all night from Columbus, Ohio, and would be meeting us in Quincy. They've worked things out so they can be with us for the rest of the trip.

Emmitt is still in high school, but this being 2020, under COVID restrictions he's able to do his schooling on the road. I can't wait to see my brother and my nephew and feel buoyed knowing we'd be four people strong again. Who knew? Sometimes fortune was on our side.

As I ride that day, my brother Brian tows a 25 foot camper (called 'The Mallard,' which we quickly renamed 'Mallory') with his Ford truck across the Midwest. Mallory is a fixer-upper Brian and his wife purchased a mere seven days ago. This is Mallory's maiden voyage and she would prove a huge asset to the second half of our trip.

Our original plan had been to go through Quincy, Missouri, but after some discussion, we feel crossing the Mississippi River would be easier in Hannibal. This is the first deviation from the original plan mapped out by my wife, Emily, and I before the trip. But I'm fine with that. From here on we'd be creating a new route each night as we'd sit in Mallory chilling and playing cards. This added a new sense of adventure and an infusion of creativity needed to get us to the finish line.

CHAPTER 19

At six foot, Brian is two inches taller than me. He's always been fit and trim and wears his sandy, blonde hair in a ponytail stuck through the back of his ball cap. Emmitt is at least an inch taller than his dad and has the same sandy blonde hair, maybe a shade darker, but it's curly and tight. He's lanky and tall and was gifted with the same creativity as his father.

They both possess an uncanny ability to problem solve on the fly, with MacGyver like finesse. They'll be perfect substitutes for Bill's role as camping scout and all around positivity spreader, and indeed would slip flawlessly into the rhythm Dave and I had built through trial and error up to this point.

Back on the road the weather is partly cloudy and cool, with very little wind, which allows me to make good time with little stress. But four days of rain and cold have me second guessing my choice to do this cockamamie adventure to begin with, so I'm a bit jumbled in my headspace. Luckily, I have been reinvigorated by the spotless and perfect upcoming forecast and the fact we'd be four people strong again at the end of the day.

Turns out Brian made good time to Missouri and arrived 12 hours early in Hannibal. He and Emmitt found a Walmart parking lot at 3 a.m. and sleep came easily for them. Dave and I weren't due to arrive until evening, so they had some time on their hands. Brian bought supplies at Walmart and Emmitt did homework on the computer. Little did they know, our journey to meet them wasn't going to happen as smoothly as we'd like.

Today was the first day I didn't wake up and head straight east on Route 36 to merely pedal until I was done. No. Up till now getting from point A to point B had been one long, straight line, but from here on out I'd have to navigate new roads with multiple route changes daily. And apparently, this was something my brain wasn't prepared to handle.

Enter 'Google Maps.'

Even on a good day, Google Maps can be a bitch and a half, but throw in brain fog, and it was damn near impossible.

Brain fog is a symptom of Ménière's that can be mildly irritating all the way to completely debilitating. Brain fog isn't just a Ménière's issue; it also affects many chronic illnesses, and attacks many people who deal with anything from cancer to depression to everything in between.

On my bike, my brain had its work cut out just keeping me upright and sane. I'm not good at multitasking and problem solving and my short-term memory is horrible. I have a hard time finishing sentences, and words and concepts can suddenly fade away in the middle of a conversation. It can be maddening.

So when Dave called me today and said to take a right off of Route 36, follow a particular road through a new town, and go down some country road after that, then take a left until I hit a major highway, then take that straight to Hannibal, you might as well have told me that I had five minutes to discover the meaning of life.

I take the right off Route 36 and for the first time in two weeks I feel unsettled with my destination. I ride five miles to a town I can't recall, and I'm immediately lost. Of course once I get into the middle of town there are plenty of road signs to help anyone get where they're going. But to me it's like reading Mandarin. My brain focus is nil and I'm confused and uncomfortable.

I park my bike at a crossroads and call Dave. After

our last and final battery change for the day, he had sped on ahead to meet Brian at the Walmart.

"I'm lost," I squeak out.

"Okay, no problem," he replies.

"I'm in the first town after taking the right turn," I say, almost in tears.

"Okay good, I drove through there 15 minutes ago, you're headed in the right direction."

I explain some landmarks around me and we decide I need to go south until I hit the next major freeway. "Take that straight into Hannibal and you'll see the Walmart on the right hand side up on the hill. You'll know you're there because the highway narrows into town. There's a stoplight, and that's where you turn right. But from where you're at now, you should soon be seeing a sign that says, 'Hannibal 10 Miles.'"

I start pedaling again but something doesn't seem quite right. I don't see anything Dave described and I should be seeing it by now. What the hell is happening? I could be in Canada for all I know. After a couple more blocks I'm second-guessing every move I make.

My anxiety begins to spike as I see a man walking towards me. I roll to a stop and get his attention.

"Can you help me? I'm headed to Hannibal."

"Oh, that's easy," and he explained the interchange again and said I'd come to it in about ten miles. I take off again.

Up until now road signs had been plentiful, if only mildly helpful, but suddenly I see nothing pointing to the highway to Hannibal. Not even a sign that said 'Hannibal 10 Miles.' There is nothing and there should be something. And worst of all, I'm not seeing anything else Dave described, no traffic light, no intersection and no shining Walmart on the hill.

I go around some random cloverleaf and ride the

shoulder of the busy freeway, mightily anticipating seeing a stoplight. It's hard to describe the situation unless you've been in it. I've been riding all day, I'm worn out, brain fog is kicking my ass and I'm literally on the edge of my seat looking with every heartbeat for a traffic light, an intersection and/or a sign that says 'Hannibal 10 Miles.'

A full hour goes by with me in this state. Needless to say, it was beyond exhausting. Eventually I came to a sign for a town I've never heard of. It sure as hell didn't say 'Hannibal,' and no road was narrowing into an intersection with a stoplight. Something had to be wrong.

I slam my brakes and call Dave again.

I describe things around me, the cloverleaf, and that I was on some sort of highway that seemed to be going on forever. "And I haven't seen any sign yet at all for Hannibal."

"Well, you seem to be going in the right direction. Maybe you just haven't gone far enough yet."

I hang up with Dave, confused and near panic. Do I keep going? I described to Dave what I was seeing and he seemed to think this was the way. I look around me. This can't be the way.

And that's the first time I pull out my phone and check Google Maps. For fuckssake, I went 15 miles in the wrong direction!

I call Dave. Before I can say a word he says, "You should be here by now."

"I went the wrong way," I say, feeling stupid. "I went 15 miles in the wrong direction."

"Do you have enough battery power to get here?" Dave enquires.

I look down. "I think so, but it'll be close. If I'm not there in an hour and a half call me."

I turn my bike around and scoot Frogger-like through heavy traffic to the opposite shoulder. I hop on and glance down at the odometer, it reads 96 miles. 'Goddamn it,' I think to myself. My lack of concentration has cost me big time. I just added 30 more miles to my day.

When all was said and done it would be 123 total miles. A new personal best and my highmark for the trip. Unfortunately it damn near came at a huge expense. My sanity. Maybe leaving my pre-planned route wasn't the brightest idea.

Now headed in the right direction, I'm making good time and close to enjoying the ride a bit when my bike triples in weight and I roll to a stop in heavy traffic on a divided highway cut-through. "Fuck!" I scream out loud.

I call Dave and give him the news. I describe where I am and he knows exactly how to find me. I hear him turn to Brian and Emmitt and say, "He's about ten miles away. I have to take him a battery. You want to go with me, Emmitt?"

Dave comes back on, "We're on our way. Are you in a safe spot?"

He must be joking. "No."

Dave:

It never occurred to me that he'd gone the wrong way. Everytime he explained where he was it seemed perfectly matched with my drive through minutes before. I was certain he must've been right behind me. The only missing piece was that he never saw the goddamned '10 miles to Hannibal' sign. But I figured he'd just passed it without seeing it—looking down, distracted with his headphones, whatever.

Emmitt and I sped ahead and soon saw Steve standing with his bike in the emergency vehicle turn around right in the middle of the busy highway.

I carefully maneuvered the van in, and figured if a cop actually came, our situation was so absurd there was no way the cop would do anything but wait us out and let us on our way. Of course, we'd tell him or her about our trip, and probably give them a flyer. We'd been doing that all the way across the country so far. In spite of Steve's more than apparent misery and frustration, Emmitt and I couldn't help but smile at the absurdity of the situation.

Then I put myself in Emmitt's shoes: Here was a teenager, not in actual physical school, with one uncle riding a bike across the country and the other trying to keep him alive as they both changed a drained E-bike battery with huge trucks whizzing by mere inches away. I thought, 'He must think his uncles are total madmen.'

And that's when the shooting started.

That's right. The shooting started. Right across from us in the woods someone was shooting a high powered rifle. 'Crack! Crack! Crack!' Of course, my first thought was, 'Holy shit! What if they decide it'd be fun to shoot at us?' I eyed the woods to see if I could make out a human. But no, just trees. 'Crack! Crack! Crack!'

It was totally unnerving, but I looked at Emmitt and we couldn't help but laugh a little. I slapped him on the back, "Well, if we get picked off, it was good knowing ya."

Battery finally in place, Steve gathered himself, nearly cracked a smile with us at the absurdity of it all, and took off wobbly and exhausted right into the middle of cars and trucks careening past him at 80 mph, mere inches off his elbow.

Emmitt and I watched a few minutes from the median and I hoped to God my nephew didn't have to witness his

126

uncle getting splattered right there and then. We hopped in the van and I glanced at Emmitt before we took off. He must think his uncles are the craziest sons of bitches in the whole world.

After 123 miles I arrive at the Walmart. Seeing the van and Mallory parked in the perfect spot settles me a bit. I slip into my camp chair under a tree and relax. I set up my tent in the grass next to the vehicles. Brian offers to have me sleep in the camper but the orange bubble has become my safe place.

I wake up a lot during the night and want to walk around when I can't sleep. So I would be the most annoying housemate ever in the camper. I never sleep well and I fidget and snore. That doesn't help. All this would best be done alone. Normally it took all the energy I had each day just to ride and meet people and pass out flyers. All I wanted to do at the end of the day was be in my tent, listening to a ball game, and knowing I wasn't disturbing anyone.

But first things first. I need to find a way to charge the batteries overnight. We had gotten creative with this challenge and tonight would be our most creative yet. After a short rest I tell Brian to follow me. There are no hookups for the camper and no outlets to be seen. It was a parking lot, for God's sake. But, while resting in my chair under a tree next to Mallory I had noticed a single story apartment complex to my right. It was down a one hundred foot embankment next to the lot. I tell Brian we are going to scramble down the hill and find an outlet. He looks at me like I'm crazy, but he needs to get his feet wet and this was a perfect initiation.

We approach the complex and notice three older women sitting on a porch, chain smoking. Two of them had cats on their laps. Living downhill from a Walmart my guess was this wasn't the first time these gals had to deal with begging riff raff from the nearby parking lot. To be honest, we were a frightening sight. Brian's long hair and me having just gotten off my bike screamed moochers. I introduce myself and notice Brian is standing a good fifteen feet behind me. Handguns aren't as accurate as people think and I could read Brian's mind: I'm probably safe back here.

I noticed walking up there was a 110 outlet next to one of the chairs being occupied.

Perfect.

After a short discussion, I send Brian back to Mallory to grab a flyer. By the time he came back, the ladies had decided to let me plug in my battery. Another miracle. They even went as far as to get a bath towel to wrap the battery so it would be sort of hidden and not have to sit on the concrete porch. They were so generous.

That night I set my alarm for 2:30 a.m. and that's when I scramble back down and switch the batteries out. In the morning I would retrace my steps to retrieve the second battery and leave them a note thanking them for graciously helping.

Tomorrow will be three miles to the bridge over the Mississippi River into Illinois. But remember, we're still in Missouri. All night cars and trucks felt the need to do the 'Missouri burnout' across the 24-hour Walmart parking lot.

What can I say, Missouri? You're something.

I'd been on a scavenger hunt for inner ear specialists in Colorado going on two years. I went everywhere and it seemed there was no way to diagnose Ménière's disease. It was a hodgepodge hit and miss exercise in futility.

An MRI ruled out a brain tumor. As I said before, I was really hoping for a tumor because they could simply remove it, then life would return to normal.

Blood work ruled out an autoimmune disease. Check that box.

I also didn't have a bone chip floating in my ear. Check that box, too.

My next specialist was an audiologist who put me through a gamut of torture tests to see if my brain was malfunctioning, or if my ear was slowly dying. This was one of the worst days of my life.

The object of the tests were to make me as sick as possible by recreating all of my symptoms at once. I was hooked up to machines that could return data on what was going on with me. I had goggles placed over my eyes and hot and cold water blasted into my ears. Then, air pulses blasted into my ears. My eyes would react in a way that told the doctor what was happening in my head. This made me extremely nauseous and so sick I vomited.

But I wasn't done yet.

She then led me weak-kneed into a round chamber painted completely black. It was an eight feet in diameter tube and there was a rotating chair in the middle. Oh, hell no, I thought. I was strapped in with my feet secured in what felt like snowboard bindings. My arms were secured to the armrests and I had two joysticks like a video game. After she locked me in and went back to her computer, her voice boomed from a speaker inside the cylinder. "I'm going to rotate you around 200 times a minute. When I tell you, you'll see two green LED lines floating in front of your eyes." It felt like I was in the worst episode of Star Trek ever. But for fuck's sake, here I go.

As promised, I started spinning. Faster and faster and faster. I was glad it was pitch dark because I knew previous riders must've splattered tons of vomit inside this cylinder of death. But soon enough, two LED laser-like lines appear out of nowhere. "I want you to use the joysticks and match the two lines up," her voice says from the darkness. Swallowing the bile in my throat, I get the job done.

I rotated to a slow stop and the door opened. I could hardly walk. We left the lab and entered her office. I collapsed in the chair opposite her. "Well, it's not your brain, so it's definitely your inner ear. There's nothing we can do for you. You'll need to see another specialist."

No, shit.

Well, ok. You're number nine. I guess now it's off to find number ten.

Dave:

I lived near Steve in Colorado when he was first diagnosed and I watched him trek around the state trying to get an answer to his condition. Oftentimes, he would know the specifics of these tests days before heading to the doctor, usually down in Denver, an hour and a half drive from where we lived.

Now, I hate going to the doctor. Let's be clear, most people do. The last time I was in the hospital for a test was when I was eight years old. So anyone who has to do a battery of tests like Steve did, especially as a full grown adult, has my admiration. It was crushing to know that as bad as he felt, he had to drive in a car an hour and a half (not fun at all when you're already carsick 24/7) only to be literally tortured into feeling even WORSE, and then having to drive back home another hour and a half (of course, his wife would drive him).

Now, when most of us are sick, we don't want to go anywhere. But if we do, we endure the torture to get ourselves to a destination that hopefully makes us better. But to do this knowing you're going somewhere they're going to make you WORSE, and then you have to endure the trip back home—I just couldn't even imagine.

I know that when life deals you a hand like this, like cancer patients doing chemo, you have to just do it. There really is no choice. But it's hard to watch someone I care about go through something like this, especially when all I could do was watch. There was nothing else I could do.

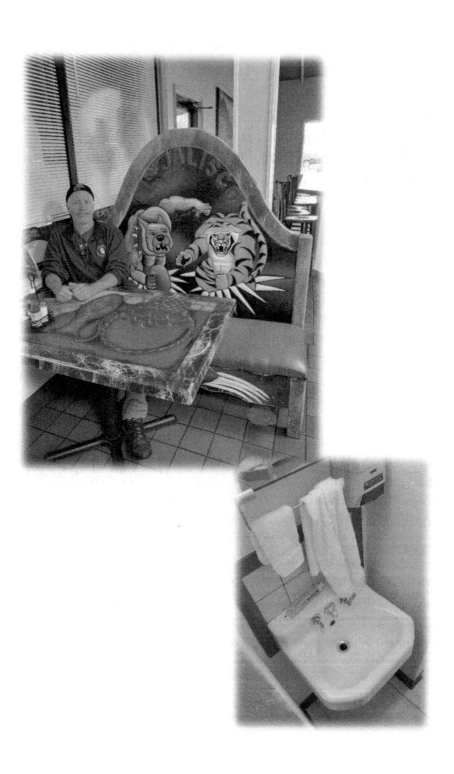

PART 5

Illinois: God's country

Hannibal, Missouri-Winchester, Illinois, 59 miles
Winchester, Illinois-Taylorville, Illinois, 70 miles
Taylorville, Illinois-Mattoon, Illinois, 66 miles

CHAPTER 20

September 14th, 2020

Day 14

After 123 miles yesterday I decided to shorten my mileage for today. We talked last night about a reasonable destination and decided on Jacksonville, Illinois. A paltry 80 miles. Piece of cake.

Last night after we plotted the route, I hit the sack a little uneasy. I'd be facing four road interchanges that I couldn't fuck up or I'd end up again wasting precious time, energy (me and my batteries), and risking my health. After yesterday's debacle, I knew concentration issues could be a problem.

The first huge obstacle would be getting me over the Mississippi River. This would entail me leaving Hannibal at sunup when traffic was light. I'd hop on Interstate 72 to cross the bridge, a major highway, then exit onto County Road 106.

That road eased my mind because it was a two lane country road and bike-friendly. I just had to get there. I could stay on that road for most of my day. As I readied myself the next morning in our makeshift Walmart camp, I passed on making the morning send off video because my anxiety and nerves were getting the better of me.

For all I knew, crossing the Mississippi on a major highway—just like back at St. Joseph—could be monumentally dangerous and spell certain death. None of us on the team knew for sure how it would go, and I didn't think it fair to family and friends to film myself 20 minutes before I died. At least that was my thought process.

We get the team together to finalize the game plan.

Now, just like back at St. Joseph, and each time we hit a potentially dangerous stretch of road, Dave offers to roll behind me in the van with flashers.

It seemed to me even more dangerous to have a van doing 15-20 mph blocking traffic going 75-80 mph as I turtled down a lane of highway, or even if the van straddled the shoulder. I didn't want the potential pileup of death to be on my conscience. And it would be. For the rest of my life. I'd rather take my chances on my own.

I tell them, "You guys stay here, I'll hit the highway and cross the bridge, and when I get to the turn off for County Road 106, I'll call and tell you I made it." They'd be able to relax, break camp, and catch up later.

As much as I'd stewed all night long and worried myself sick the whole way to the bridge, to my surprise I cross the river without a hitch. Since it's Sunday morning, traffic is light and I arrive at my turnoff feeling fresh, victorious and relieved. But, still, anxiety is a bitch. I can overwhelm myself for no reason. The MD Monster is always lurking and second-guessing my future. It's a constant battle. So once I'm on County Road 106, I pull over and call the boys.

I can tell from their voices they're glad to hear I

had conquered the bridge. I tell them I regretted not wearing our GoPro camera on my head because the bridge, the lighting with the sun just peeking up and a wisp of fog covering the mighty river were majestic and awe inspiring. Still by far one of my favorite scenes from the trip, if not number one itself.

Out on Route 106, I sign off with the boys, put on my music and start pedaling. I didn't know till later that the team had decided to re-enact my bridge crossing; GoPro and all. Dave strapped the GoPro on his head and Brian and Emmett followed in the van.

The Mississippi River that divides America neatly in two is one of the largest rivers in the world. Their choice to record crossing over it made me so happy. I missed my chance, but they knew it meant something to me. I'm so glad they did it.

The sun is up now, bright and full, and I ride straight into it. The warmth on my face feels great and I relax into a rhythm. For the first time on the trip, I'm on a very rural road for a long duration. Route 36 across Kansas was rural, yet still wide and spacious. Route 106 is rural, but quite narrow and winding. Trees, houses, yards and ditches are snug up against me, and it gives a slight claustrophobic feeling. But still fantastic.

I love these country two-lane roads with the corn stalks so close I can reach out and run my hand through the foliage. I do this often and it always seems to tamp my anxiety, if only for a little while. Because true, I don't have much of a shoulder to ride on, maybe ten inches to the right of the white line, but I don't mind. I can see cars approaching in my rearview mirror and for the most part they give me plenty of room. Moving into the opposite lane when appropriate, they give me even more space. I'd always throw a quick wave of appreciation when someone moved over and more often than not got a return wave or quick beep of a horn.

In my bright yellow safety vest, and being in the middle of nowhere, those motorists knew I was in it for the long haul. I was on an epic ride and they honked, knowing it would encourage me to keep pedaling. This happened many times a day, and it always felt great. The people of middle America constantly surprised me with their generosity and positive attitudes.

The downfall today was that I spent so much energy worrying about the bridge crossing that I didn't think I could make it to Jacksonville. I call Dave and say we need to shorten my day. I'm still paying the price for four days in the Missouri rain and my 123 mile debacle the day before.

The good news is that by crushing so many 100 mile days up till then, we are way ahead of schedule just as I hoped we'd be. I pull over in a dirt patch to drop a deuce in a cornfield and check my Google Maps. For some reason, the town of Winchester, Illinois stood out. Jacksonville is definitely too far, but I feel good about Winchester. I call Dave. "I can't make it to Jacksonville, so have Brian look at Winchester."

Dave:

Brian had already been scouting ahead and was sitting in a Walmart parking lot in Pittsfield, Illinois. I rang him up. "How's Pittsfield look?" I asked.

"We went through it and came back. It's pretty big."

"Will it work for tonight?"

"Yeah, I don't see why not."

"Well . . . " I hesitated, "for some reason Steve wants Winchester. Can you roll ahead and look in Winchester?"

Now, this conversation with Brian might seem a little odd, since by the time I rolled through Pittsfield, I realized Brian had been right. Pittsfield was much, much bigger than I gave it credit for on the map. And not only would camping be amply available, he was already sitting in a Walmart parking lot that would suffice just fine.

But Steve was, in a word, or two, oddly, maybe even bizarrely, obsessed with Winchester. In my few conversations with him that day, he would literally say, "What about Winchester? What do you think about Winchester? I think we should go to Winchester. Have Brian look at Winchester." And I'd say a few words and he'd go, "I think Winchester. We should look at Winchester." To the point where I was thinking, Oh, my God. I'll do anything if you just stop saying the word 'Winchester!'

Now, it's not like Steve is Rain Man or anything, and he wasn't suffering any mental issues on this trip that I was aware of, but those few conversations were definitely . . . definitely . . . those conversations were definitely . . . the most odd of the trip. I resigned myself to his obsession with Winchester, so I rolled through Pittsfield and on to . . . I can't even say it.

But the thing is, and to this day I don't know how Steve knew, or if he himself even knew at the time, but rolling into Winchester was going to change our trip in a way none of us could have ever imagined.

In a 100 percent positive way.

CHAPTER 21

Dave:

Brian dutifully rolled ahead to Winchester and I rolled out of Pittsfield wondering if we'd made a mistake and despite Steve's Rain Man obsession with Winchester, we might end up backtracking to Pittsfield after all. But I rolled into Winchester and found the town square. I was trying to call Brian to meet up with him wherever he may be, but he was not answering his phone. 'That's odd,' I thought. So, it being a gorgeous fall day, I parked the van in the town square and explored a little.

I learned from a plaque in the middle of the square that the courthouse in Winchester was where Lincoln and Douglass had one of their first public debates over an important piece of legislation. 'Interesting,' I thought, being a lover of history.

The town square was, well, small, so I rounded it in no time and just before I jumped in the van, I spotted Brian's camper go by out on the main road. I quickly made a couple turns to head him off going a back way. I came down an alley next to a church just as he was coming toward me. We passed each other then he looped back around and we parked in the street.

"How did you know we were here?" Brian asked, incredulous and laughing.

"Well, I was over in the town square trying to call you and saw you go by, so I came over."

He was still laughing at the seeming coincidence and informed me that he'd gone inside the church we were next to about an hour ago. It was letting out (it was Sunday morning, after all) and he decided to see if he could track down the pastor.

Now, one of the things we'd discussed before the trip as far as places we could stay cheap or for free was to ask churches along the way if they'd let us set up in their parking lot for the night, then we'd roll on the next morning, no fuss, no muss. That was before we knew Walmarts allow overnight parking, of course, so between that and camping sites across Kansas and a smattering of hotels in Missouri, we hadn't had occasion yet for the church idea. But now we did. And the first church Brian went in welcomed us with open arms.

I was a bit fuzzy from lack of sleep and my own night-long-into-morning anxiety about Steve crossing the bridge over the Mississippi that morning, so I looked at Brian and said, "You did what? You and Emmitt just drove by and saw people coming out of this church and you guys walked in and talked to the pastor?"

"Yeah, and he's super cool and letting us stay here tonight."

I was incredulous. It was that easy? Just like that? First church he tried? Well, hell yeah, let's do it. "What do we do now?"

"Park in the back and set up our stuff."

"And this guy is cool with that?"

"Yeah," Brian said, as if it was obvious. "Wait till you meet him."

Robin Lyons is the pastor of the Winchester United Methodist church and when he stood in the pulpit that day he had no idea he was on a collision course with the steam-roller that was 'Ménière's: On the VertiGO!'

I was 15 miles out from Winchester when Dave called. "Brian and Emmitt found a church and talked to the pastor. He seems cool with us staying overnight in his parking lot and is willing to let us charge the batteries in

141

his church. He's also printed off 30 more flyers for us in his office." We'd started the trip with 30 flyers and we were down to one. This was great news.

"I just got here," Dave says. "This guy's super cool and wants to buy us lunch at a local diner when you get here."

Hot diggity dog, I'm thinking. A place to stay and lunch too? This is too much! Dave gives me directions and I call my dad to help me get over the final five mile hump. I find the Methodist Church with no problems and it feels right.

I meet Robin and he is exactly as Dave described, super cool. He is very down to earth and had a great spirit about him.

We become instant friends and he can't wait to find out more about our trip. I mean, how many times do four wild, homeless looking dudes roll into his church parking lot on a sunny Sunday afternoon? And not only that, they say they need help. The population being under 1,500 the chances were probably nil something like this would ever happen. But without batting an eye, this man took us under his wing, literally, and never stopped giving to us, serving us, and encouraging us until we left. It was the most incredible thing.

And we learn about him too, his life, his work, his son, his church and his town. It also doesn't take long for the whole city to learn that Robin had taken in four wackadoodles and is letting them camp behind his church.

It is a Sunday so Robin has church issues to deal with. He gives us directions to a local diner and says he just called ahead. "They are expecting you guys. Order whatever you want, I'm paying," he told us.

We do just that, and return to the church with full bellies.

I pitch my tent in a grassy area between the church and Robin's house and we spend the rest of the day chatting and getting to know each other.

That evening I wasn't sure if I should push our luck, but I take a chance and say, "Robin, you've been nice to us and given us lunch and a place to stay and everything, but I was wondering if we could stay another night so I can have a rest day tomorrow."

The man doesn't even hesitate. "Of course," he responds. "On top of that you can use the church facilities whenever you want and I'm going to buy you all pizza tomorrow night as well."

We thank him profusely, tell him he really doesn't have to buy us pizza, he's done enough already, but he instantly felt like a long, lost Schwier brother for someone we'd only known a couple hours.

We broke up the chat and Brian gets busy hardwiring his camper into an external outlet from the church while Dave does our social media at a table in the church cafeteria.

I was feeling good knowing I'd be able to sit in the shade of the steeple the next day charging my bike batteries while recharging my own inner batteries. It had been a great day beyond what I could've ever imagined. I mean, it was only that morning I thought I might be fighting for my life over the Mississippi River. But now as the sun put itself to bed I feel much more relaxed. I listen to two entire baseball games on the radio until I grow fidgety.

It's after midnight but I go inside the church to sit in the quiet of the sanctuary. Well, it would've been quiet to anyone without a ringing ear, but tonight I don't let that bother me. I thank God. I thank God that we'd gotten this far safely. I thank God for my family and friends. I sit in the still silence for over an hour, and as I head back out to my orange bubble I notice my battery charging on the floor in the entryway of the church. It's fully charged so I switch out the other battery, and silently thank God for that, too.

I awake in the morning in a dry cocoon surrounded by a sea of wet. "What the . . . ?" It was then I realize that I'd left the rain cover off the orange bubble and the dew had settled in and soaked everything in my tent. Luckily it hadn't been enough to penetrate my blankets. Dammit. Gotta remember to put that thing on each night.

Anyway, it's another gorgeous day so I set up my camp chair and barely move all day. Aaaaaah. A whole day off. It's exactly what I need and I take full advantage of it.

Robin treats us to lunch again and asks if we could take some pictures for his church newsletter. Of course, we agree, after all, we need shots for our social media too.

He tells me he has a friend who writes for the local newspaper and asks if I'd be willing to be interviewed? I don't hesitate. "Absolutely, let's do it. It'd be an honor."

Later that afternoon I do an interview over the phone with Carmen Ensinger from the *Scott County Times* with Dave sitting beside me. Carmen and I hit it off instantly and spend more time laughing and telling stories than talking about my trip. It was a hoot and exactly the kind of thing I was hoping for on this trip in terms of raising awareness of Ménière's Disease. How did we get so lucky? (Two weeks later the article came out and it was fantastic.)

True to his word, as we're wrapping the interview, Robin calls out from his office. "What kind of pizza do you like?" Jesus, and I mean the real Jesus, thank you for this man and his hospitality. In no time we're munching pepperoni and cheese on benches near the church entrance as board members late for a meeting stop by to warmly greet us and ask about our trip.

Over pizza Robin laments not being able to have me speak at the church Sunday morning. "Everyone would've really enjoyed that," he tells us, and I still can't believe this man's kindness and hospitality.

The next day, it's tough leaving Winchester. We'd found a family here. A true home.

We're halfway through the trip and I'd been away from my wife and son for more than two weeks. The upcoming thought of being on my bike for hours on end by myself gave me an empty feeling. I ready myself and my bike and ask Robin if he'd do a joint morning send-off video with me for social media. "Sure, but I'm not sure how good I'll be," he demures.

"You'll be great," we assure him, and he was. It was perfect.

Afterwards Robin asks where we're heading, and we tell him Taylorville. He says, "Hang on a second, I'll call Rebecca, she's a pastor there. I'll tell her about you guys and she might let you stay in her church parking lot tonight."

Brian, Dave and I look at each other, again, hardly able to believe what we're hearing. This would be a huge weight off our day knowing we'd have a safe, secure destination for the night.

Robin walks back out and says Rebecca would be glad to accept us with open arms. So Brian grabs Dave's borrowed bike and Robin walks us to the road while Emmitt hangs back doing homework in the camper.

I feel great and rejuvenated. My symptoms are at a minimum and we'd made some great, new friends.

Thank you, Robin Lyons. You are one of a kind, my brother. Exceptional indeed.

As Brian and I pedal out of Winchester I hold a sad heart but with a smile. Our time in Winchester was much more than a rest day and some good meals. It was strangers helping strangers. It was bonding at a moment's notice in the oddest of circumstances. It was humanity at its best. And I was just as refreshed by that as the down time in my chair.

The weather is optimal and my destination is set. As Brian peels off and heads back the way we came, I chose Mark Knopfler's solo music to be my companion. My bike and I feel as one unit. I'd learned to read the cornstalks to gauge wind direction. I could switch gears and settings without looking down. I was supremely confident in my ability and the ability of the team. The way everything is coming together is too good to be true, I think to myself with a smile, as I ride mile after mile down beautiful country roads.

Little did I know the Monster was closing in, hiding in the bushes, lurking and ready to attack with all its might in a way I hadn't previously experienced on the trip.

The best day quickly morphed into my worst nightmare.

CHAPTER 22

The problem with Ménière's is you are always second-guessing what you're doing. As in, 'My ears are ringing louder today, did I eat too much salt?' Or, 'The pressure in my ear is full and my eyes are bugging out, did I read ebooks on my phone too long?' Or, 'I'm dizzy and nauseous and need my cane for support; did the one and a half hour drive to Denver cause this?'

That's what Ménière's does to you, and why anxiety plays such an essential role. You never know when things are going to go south. And you never know why you have good days, either. It's all a guessing game. That's why I never want to leave my bed.

I hate thinking about all the things that *might* happen if I get up and do something. After eight years of tit-for-tat anxiety, I learned long ago that the Monster has its own timetable and little did I know as I pedaled toward Taylorville that my clock was ticking.

I left Winchester hours ago feeling good. If I wasn't running my hands through corn stalks, I was pedaling parallel to train tracks. I passed grain silos and bored cows uninterested in my travels. I could be there or not and it wouldn't change a frickin' thing. The crops would still grow. The horses and cattle would be no better off because I rode by and gave them a wave. The trains would still move slowly delivering their cargo to the next town whether I was riding by or not. I suddenly felt a sense of smallness. But strangely, in the same moment came an inexplicable feeling of peace. After all, I was only responsible for me, myself, and I right then. What else could I do?

A trance comes over me and I get lost in my rhythm. As I pass another corn field I think, sure I have a chronic illness, but today I can live with it. This isn't so bad. Ouch. Bam! Wrong answer. Because you can never predict the Monster.

The second you let your guard down, somehow it knows. And it doesn't want me to have a good day. It never wants me to have a good day. It tries to talk me into staying in bed all day or not leaving the couch for days on end. It says "Sure, go to the store, you'll be miserable!" And, "Sure, take the dog for a walk, you'll get back and have to rest for an hour!" It's a constant mind-fuck of anticipation and fear.

So enjoying today's ride is an anomaly. The sun feels great with the perfectly cool air. My life isn't so bad, I think. At least I get to ride on a nice day like this (a thought that never crossed my mind in 100-degree Kansas or 45 degree, rainy Missouri.)

I am ignorantly and naively enjoying my day, but in retrospect I realize I'm a dipshit. MD always drops the other foot. Always. And by the end of today his boot'd be straight up my ass. I should know better by now.

Dave calls and says he and Brian are in Taylorville. Again, the church was right off the town square and easy to find. He, Brian, and Emmitt are going to walk to a nearby burger joint for a late lunch. I end the call and think, ok, right off the town square. That's easy. I'll just ride to the town square and figure it out from there.

Dave:

I got into Taylorville right after Brian and Emmitt so they had already effectively 'checked us in' with the church and I quickly found their camper parked out back.

I parked the van next to it and thought, 'Where's Brian?' Nowhere to be found. But I tracked them down over on the town square eating in a cramped little burger joint that seemed, if not currently in the process of being shut down by the health department, that it sure as hell needed an inspection.

"This place is awesome!" Brian chirped as I walked in. He and Emmitt damn near have their knees pushing up their chins as they munched cheeseburgers at the smallest diner table and chairs I'd ever seen.

I looked at him. "You recommend it?"

"Yeah!"

Emmitt looked happy too, and I grabbed one of his fries. Mmmmmm. Ok, well, here goes nothing . . .

"There's nowhere for me to sit," I observed. "Should I just order?"

Brian, who seems to be somewhat friendly with Flo and Mel behind the counter, piped up, "We're almost done, so we'll get his to go."

Flo turned to me, "What'll you have, honey?" I got a basic cheeseburger and fries and we went out and sat at a table, bigger this time, along the side of the building.

"Oh, my God!" I exclaimed after chomping a huge hack of burger. "That's amazing!"

"Told ya," Brian chirps and Emmitt smiles.

I shrugged and flipped a fry into my mouth, "Who knew?"

When I got done eating we started walking back across the town square toward the church. But instead of turning left, we turned right when we saw the clock-tower of the courthouse on the center lawn and right across from it . . . a movie theater straight out of the 50s.

"You know what this is?" Brian asked, getting excited.

I'd seen it immediately. "The exact town square from Back to the Future!" (It looked so identical we'd later have people ask if it was the actual site of Back to the Future, but it wasn't. Back to the Future was filmed on the backlot of Universal in Los Angeles.)

Brian and I were jacked about the video possibilities for social media. I moved right, closer toward the movie theatre. Brian moved left to get an angle on the courthouse and suddenly I saw Steve come out of nowhere, flying towards Brian, and yelling about something.

Brian pointed in the direction of the church and Steve slammed the breaks, slid a burning back-tire 180, and took off.

What the hell? I jogged over. Whatever just happened, this wasn't good. I reached Brian. "What's going on?"

"I have no idea. He just asked me where the church was and took off."

By the time I enter the town square I can't see and can barely keep myself on the bike. I feel like I'm dying, and there isn't a damn thing I can do about it. This was no joke. And I'm not overexaggerating in the least.

On the edge of town I arrive at the T where Dave said to go right. 'This would get you to the town center,' he'd said. I made the right and that's when I felt it. There's no other feeling like it. "Fuck," I say out loud to no one but my bike. Fuck, not now. Fuck, not now. This can't be happening! Maybe my wishy-washy head will clear somehow? Maybe my hot sweats were simply the result of too much sun that day? Maybe my headphones had been clamping down on my ears too tight for too long? But as much as I'd love to believe any of that, deep down I know it is here. There was no way of rationalizing it. I'd only be lying to myself. It is here and it isn't going away. I still have two miles to the town center, but I'm going into a full-blown vertigo attack.

My vision is blurry as I blow through stoplights. Cars screech to a halt to avoid this crazed asshole who thinks he owns the road. At that point I'm so disoriented

I don't know if I'll even recognize the town center if I manage to get there. And most likely I won't get there. I'm in heavy afternoon traffic in a town I don't know and any second I could lose control and just smash into anything in front of me, moving or not.

I carelessly careen through three more stop signs without looking left or right. Stopping is impossible and completely out of the question. I had to take my chances. 'Keep your head still and keep riding,' I tell myself. I blast through a fourth stop sign and catch Brian out of the corner of my eye. He is smiling and waving. But I am not.

I speed past him, yelling "Where's the church?" I'm not sure he understood my urgency but his face dropped.

He points and yells, "Take the next left and go a block!" But I'm already 20 yards past him having done a total Evel Kneivel 180 slide I'd never be able to accomplish on a good day. But this wasn't a good day. It was absolute desperation.

I careen through the stop sign at the corner and drive wildly out of control in the direction Brian told me. 'I'm not going to make it,' I think, I'm not going to make it another block. 'I should just stop and lay down,' I consider. But I dig deep and talk myself into one more block. One more block.

My brain is quickly shutting down and all my faculties with it. My head is down and sweat is pouring off my face. My back and neck are covered in perspiration. I can't go any further. I'm endangering everyone in front of me and I'm sure as hell endangering myself.

I spot a church but by then I'm so disoriented I don't know if it's the right one. I just hope to God it's the one. I fly into the church and float around the side of the building. I see Brian's camper—well, sort of. My eye nystagmus is going full-on crazy. Everything is spinning in circles and my eyes are racing to keep up.

I slam to a stop and somehow put my kickstand down (probably more from muscle memory than intent at that point). I unclip my ass bag and drop it at my feet in a shady spot behind the camper. This will be my pillow no matter how uncomfortable it is. I collapse, bruising my elbow and the right side of my body, but I'm done. I was there and I'd made it.

Fuck you, Ménière's, for ruining what was up to now a fantastic day. This was the best day I'd had on my bike since Denver and you ruined it! For Whom the Bell Tolls—and my time was up. The Monster had thrown a haymaker and it landed solid. I wouldn't be getting up from the pavement for who knows how long.

Dave:

On the walk back, Brian and I have no idea what's going on. The only thing I could think was there was something we were supposed to have done and hadn't, and it threw Steve off or made things more difficult for him. We hadn't exactly pulled off a pristine trip. There were times when we as a team failed to do what needed to be done. There were times when we did actually make things harder for him and his trip. But I couldn't for the life of me think what I could've done that day.

We rounded the church and I knew immediately. Steve was curled up in a fetal position on the hot pavement of the church parking lot, right behind Brian's camper with only his ass bag for a pillow.

A full-on vertigo attack.

Now, you have to understand, before the trip, when I was even considering whether to do the trip or not, I had figured that I'd need to help Steve through a vertigo attack . . . or two . . . or three . . . or twenty. I'd already envisioned times when I'd sit with him for hours or days or however long it took for the attack to come and go. But so far he'd been so (relatively) healthy, nothing could've been further from my mind as he ran up on Brian in the town square. It caught me, and all of us I think, completely off guard. But now we needed to go into full-on triage.

CHAPTER 23

One minute feels like an hour. One hour feels like a day feels like a month feels like a year. This is where vertigo takes you. You disappear from your surroundings. Time and space become fantasy.

I've used this term earlier, time and space. It's a big part of my existence now. How long things take and how comfortable I am in the space I'm in. It took me years and hundreds of vertigo attacks to learn this hard lesson: When the Beast throws this punch, the heaviest of blows, a vertigo attack, don't fight back. Trying to keep track of how long I've been lying still during any given attack only makes it worse. Trying to stop the world from spinning and feel like I'm grounded is a waste of energy. You have to surrender with everything you have or it becomes worse. Trying to think straight is a practice in futility. Vertigo attacks are the only time where I force myself to give up completely and the Monster wins.

I will fight it at first because I need to find a safe comfortable place to float away. But once I know I'm safe and not going to endanger myself or someone else, I give in and crumble into suffering. I might have to pull my car over in a parking lot, or stumble out of a friend's house at a get-together, or in this case, find the energy to ride my bike through traffic and get to our camping spot for the night.

The aftermath can be even more devastating. For hours I'll fight to keep my sanity and even though I've been laying perfectly still, I'm depleted of every ounce of energy. But eventually I do sit up, slowly. I usually put two feet on the floor to see if I'm back in the real world. If this doesn't cause me to vomit, I sit for minutes or an hour trying to adjust to being human again.

I just took a journey to some very dark places where nothing stands still. Nothing is solid or permanent. My bed has been sideways trying to roll me off for hours. Can I just sit here and find my legs again? Can I stand up now without falling into the wall, or God forbid, find the corner of my dresser with my forehead or face? It happens.

Sometimes after an attack I'm shocked to find out I've been spinning and floating for twelve hours or more. Even up to 24 hours.

Many nights I lay in bed wishing for death, for the Grim Reaper to just grab my shaky, sweaty, spinning body and carry me over the river Styx so I can forget I was ever there.

Ménière's sufferers have 'good days' and bad days, but a vertigo attack is a horror show beyond Stephen King's worst nightmare.

Simply put, it's pure hell.

Dave:

As mentioned earlier, Brian and I had seen Steve in a full-on attack at our friend's New Year's party in Colorado. We'd carried him to the car and sent him on his way home, leaving his wife to deal with him. But now, we'd have to deal with this right in front of us. Right here in the back of some random church parking lot in Taylorville, Illinois.

I leaned over Steve. He told me, "If anyone sees me and tries to call 911, tell them not to. That's the worst thing that could happen right now."

Ménière's people know going to the ER does not do a bit of good. The doctors don't know what to do with them and whatever they try to do only makes things worse. Ménière's sufferers know this is their lot in life, and they just have to ride it out.

"What do you need?" I asked Steve.

"Nothing. I just have to lie here." I knew he couldn't move even if he wanted to. "Hand me a phone. I'm going to record this."

I reached in my pocket and handed him the phone I'd been using for social media videos. Without moving, he eked out, "Help me push 'record' and tell me when it's on." I hit record and positioned his hand in place so he didn't have to move. Eyes closed, he started a monologue describing exactly what was happening and how he was feeling. I was amazed he had the mental wherewithal to pull this off. But he knew better than I that this was one of the main reasons we were here, on this trip. For exactly this right here.

At one point he said to the camera, "This is what eye nystagmus is," and opened his eyes. His eyes darted back and forth so fast they looked like they were looping around inside his head and coming back around. It was hard to watch and I had to look away for a second.

"My eyes are trying to follow what my brain thinks is happening," he told the camera. "My brain thinks I'm spinning so my eyes are trying to help me out by keeping up. It's involuntary and I can't stop it. And it can go on for hours."

'God, I hope not,' I thought. How can he stand that? He finished the video and told me to post it as soon as possible.

I'm concerned it'd be borderline exploitation to do so, but as he said, it was part of what we were out here to do, if not the main thing.

He saw me hesitate. "This is the real deal. If I can't be real, then what am I doing out here?" Again he had a point and his bravery inspires me. I do my part to kick Ménière's in the nuts and click the video up to social media.

Oh, my God, it occurs to me, what's going to happen

when our close friends and family see that? The guy looks like he's dying!

Brian and Emmitt were in the camper scrambling to toss things around and tidy up. Brian poked his head out. "Does he want to come in here?"

I said back, "He can't move. He might be there awhile."

But Steve surprised me and said, "Yeah, I'll go in."

I knew from the last attack I witnessed we'd have to bodily carry him into the camper.

"Brian, come on out," I barked.

Emmitt came out first so I gave him the phone and told him to film. Brian came around and we lifted Steve under his arms. We got him halfway up and he said, "I have to rest my head a second," and planted his head straight into the back of the camper. With his head still, he got his legs under him and said, "OK, let's go." And Brian and I basically poured him onto the couch in the camper.

"Do you want the air conditioner on?" Brian asked.

"Yeah," Steve eked. "Brian, get your phone and text everyone that I'm OK and I want radio silence for the rest of the day."

Brian understood and jumped out of the camper with his phone as I began to ask Steve questions about what he was feeling. "Save it," he told me. "Ask me on camera and we'll record it."

Emmitt handed my phone back and we made three short videos of me asking Steve questions about his experience. This we also put on social media along with Emmitt's video of Brian and me carrying him into the camper. For the record, the vertigo videos did get a lot of views, of course, but so far I'd only posted them to Instagram and Facebook.

A few days later Steve would ask, "Did you post that video of me laying on the pavement behind the camper to

YouTube?"

I told him, "No, I haven't."

To my mind, I didn't think it'd matter that much. People had followed that part of the trip, watched those videos when we posted them, and now we'd moved on to other things. But I did as he asked, since, after all, this was his trip. For perspective, up till then the most views one of our YouTube videos had gotten was 126 in two months. We thought that was a big deal. The pavement video had 800 views in two days, and to this day is well over a thousand.

The boy was right again. Great call.

Steve knows the Ménière's community well. I was an outsider. Even after eight years, I was still learning. And there'd be oh, so much more to learn. I had no idea after this massive vertigo attack that this was still just the beginning.

Lying on the pavement behind the camper, I am bruised and starting to give in to the fight. This fight I will lose and I know it. The parking lot is hard and my brain is telling me the pavement is slanted at a 45 degree angle. 'Don't fight it,' I say to myself. 'Just roll with it.' Maybe I could just roll like a ship right off the edge of the world dropping into outer space?

Since time stands still during an attack, I quickly have no idea how long I've been lying behind the camper, I have no idea how much time passed before the boys arrived. I am aware of their presence but nothing is making sense.

I raise my arm slowly straight up. I say I want to film this and post it. Someone hands me the phone, and I ask for the video to be turned on. I hope my face is center screen, but I have no way to tell.

I open my eyes to explain what's happening, but my eye nystagmus is full-on. This means that when I open them, everything I see is spinning quickly before my eyes. When this happens it's impossible to focus and my eyes automatically try to track my environment. It's a horrible feeling and hard to do without throwing up.

I finish the video and decide I need to get off the concrete and onto a soft couch in the camper. I might've been like that for hours (who knew?) and I'd rather be on something soft than the concrete parking lot. Since I have no sense of right side up or upside down, I need assistance.

I have to talk myself into moving at all, really, because this is an anxiety like no other. You have to understand—I'd rather die than sit up. Sitting up will cause the world to spin more violently than it already is, and if it changes direction I will definitely start vomiting. Just the thought is paralyzing and scary. I always cry at this point. I'm terrified to move.

I explain to Dave my plan to get into the camper through tears of humiliation. Dave and Brian will next have to reach under my arms and support me into the camper and to the cushioned bench. After a couple minutes of inner argument, I force myself upright. I fall headfirst into the back of the camper and rest my head on the cool bumper. Step one completed.

I wait for myself to steady a bit. The feeling of time is slipping away. How long have I been in this position? Minutes? An hour? I fantasize about running to Brian's truck and backing over myself to make this all stop.

Emmitt records Dave and Brian struggling to pour me into the camper and it ends up being the most watched video of the trip to that point. I'm not talking viral numbers such as a cat playing the piano or some shit, but it was viewed over 10,000 times around the world on our social media sites.

That may sound awesome to most people, but I

was ashamed and embarrassed. Losing all of your cognitive abilities is not something to be proud of. It's also something most people have never seen. It's scary to watch. And many Ménière's sufferers said they had to turn it off. Others said they cried through the whole episode. These people knew exactly what I was feeling and it's beyond heartbreaking to watch.

I finally get inside the camper and flop onto a padded bench. Dave and I make a couple videos explaining my situation and after that I surrender. I put my cold-snap towel over my face and let vertigo carry me away.

You may think I'm being a bit overdramatic, but let me tell you, I'm not. I'm not even coming close to explaining what this actually feels like. There are no words. A vertigo attack is intangible. It has no timeline. It's just pure suffering that can't be explained with words. How can you describe the indescribable? I'm trying my best to do it here anyway.

There are thousands of people experiencing vertigo attacks around the world as I write this, and my heart goes out to each and every one of them. If there's any good thing that could come from my humiliation and pain, it'd be to let other Ménière's sufferer's know this, and to feel it deep in their bones: You are not alone. There are others of us out here and we are with you.

You are not alone.

CHAPTER 24

A lot of people think they have the answers to my chronic illness and I've heard them all.

'If you just exercise more, you'll be healthier.'

Okay, stop right there. I just rode a bike over 900 miles in two weeks.

'If you ate more, you'd make yourself feel better.'

Let's stop right there again. What if I put you in a car and we drove for hours on the California Pacific Highway, up and down and around one bend after another until you get so carsick you begged me to pull over and stop. But instead I speed up and make you feel even worse. Now you're pleading for your life, "Please, please, pull over and stop the car! I can't take this anymore, I'm going to die!" But we're going to keep going, and oh, by the way, if you eat this greasy, rare, steak with greasy fried eggs on top, you'll feel much better. Oh, and top that off with a warm stick of butter. Just cram it down your throat, you'll feel better.

Living with a chronic illness is survival. I will do anything I need to do to survive. If that means lying on my couch for a week straight, then so be it.

What I'm saying is Ménière's Disease is trickier to navigate than people think. Ménière's symptoms are far and wide. No one knows what causes it and no one knows how to cure it . . . yet. Each person has a varying degree of symptoms to manage. Every one of us suffers differently. There are no foolproof answers, just improvised ways and means to mitigate symptoms. This is my journey I'm sharing, and I'm hoping someone out there can relate somewhat. But I don't know how to fix anyone. I don't have any answers. And neither does anyone else. Find out what works for you and manage the best you can.

The question I'm most often asked is, "What's

your best advice for someone with Ménière's Disease?" Here's my answer, and it's the only advice I ever give: Find a good doctor. A doctor who cares about your case. A doctor who is sympathetic to your plight. My first nine specialists didn't do dick for me. But I kept searching. Number Ten was like hitting the lottery. Dr. Robert Muckle with the Denver Ear Associates at the Swedish Medical Center in Denver invested the time and energy to help me. He was my game changer. So finding the right doctor is crucial. Enough said.

I've had vertigo attacks lasting more than eight hours, some lasting twenty four or more. Usually I can't stand up for the next day or so. The attack in Taylorville was less than three hours, thank God—one of the shortest attacks I've ever experienced. But still, I was completely wiped out. Returning to Planet Earth takes time.

By evening in Taylorville I'm sitting up and sipping water. At home I would stay in bed the entire next day recovering, but I decide to ride my bike tomorrow instead. This is my game, my rules. In order to do this, I would need to eat and get my energy back.

I mop myself up and Brian, Dave, and Emmitt ready themselves to scout for food. Cindy, the church secretary, meets us as we walk across the parking lot. She tells us a good friend of hers has Ménière's and asks if we would be interested in meeting with her tonight? I told her, "Of course."

Before the trip Dave and I thought it'd be a good idea to interview people across the country in person about their experiences with Ménière's. Meeting John on day one was a great start, and here was another opportunity. We schedule a meeting for later that night.

After everything that's happened today, meeting a stranger and carrying on a filmed interview will be difficult, to say the least. But that's why I'm out here. I have one month with my rules and my show, and I'm not letting this opportunity pass.

But first, I need to eat and rest a bit. We grab a bite at an Italian bistro on the town square. I stuff myself with chicken parm and pasta. I need to get as much protein, starches, and carbs as I can get. I'm in unchartered territory wanting to be so active right after an attack. I might be pushing myself too hard, but I feel I have no choice. It's simply the next step in the journey.

Walking back to the church at dusk, the boys say they still want to do their *Back to the Future* remake for social media. "That would be great," I tell them, "just count me out. I need to rest."

"We just need you for one scene," they say. "To ride your bike across the square, then you can go rest while we finish it."

I reluctantly agree, buoyed by the fact that the setting was perfect. I ride my bike twice past Dave's camera and leave them to finish the project. Emmitt plays crazy Doc Emmett Brown and he's fantastic.

Cindy and her friend Sue Endsley show up as the boys return from filming. Pastor Rebecca also comes out of the church to meet us for the first time. She is very nice, full of hospitality, and allows us to use a meeting room in the church for the interview.

The room has thick, plush, red carpet and dark wood molding everywhere. A giant dark polished table sits in the middle of the room. It looks like The Declaration of Independence could've been signed here. Amazing.

At the other end of the room we see two red, plush couches framed by a fireplace. Perfect.

Dave sets up the GoPro on an end table and off we go. I have no idea what I said or if it was even coherent,

I'm trusting Dave for that. All I know is how amazing it is to meet my second person ever that suffers the same cruel disease I do.

Dave:

When we got back from filming in the town square, Steve was sitting in his chair outside the camper, eyes closed, resting his head. I looked to my left and saw Cindy and Sue Endsley park their car and begin to walk toward us.

"Oh my God," I thought. "I forgot about the interview. This day has held enough activity for a week, and we're going to do more?" I looked at my brother. "You know you don't have to do this. They will understand."

He answered with eyes closed. "No, I want to. This is what we're out here for, this stuff right here. Besides, we only have one chance to do this, so let's go."

Cindy and Sue greeted us warmly and just like meeting John back in Denver, Steve and Sue immediately bonded over Ménière's horror stories. I couldn't pull the camera out fast enough and began filming right there in the back parking lot.

After a few minutes, we shuffled into the church where we could've interrupted Ben Franklin and Thomas Jefferson having a fireside chat. The room was incredible. The perfect setting for this interview.

I hit 'record' and sat back fighting nightmares of later finding nothing had recorded. I glanced nervously at Brian a couple times and shrugged my shoulders. After a couple minutes the blinking light on the GoPro, as well as the screen, goes to sleep. We had no idea if it was still recording. But that quickly faded as the intensity of Steve and Sue's conversation took over the room.

I was instantly transported to another world. Their

world. The world of the daily Ménière's sufferer. That moment on the trip will stick with me for the rest of my life. It wasn't just a matter of confirming everything Steve had been telling us through the mouth of Sue Endsley. It was more than that. It was hearing two people speak about the most horrendous suffering, and yet, living with it with an indescribable grace, resilience and light–heartedness that only these two could have pulled off in that moment.

When I clicked the camera off after an hour Brian and I knew we'd just witnessed something otherworldly, and made comments to each other along those lines. I knew in that moment how valuable this would be not only for people with Ménière's, but especially for those without. There wasn't a stone Steve and Sue had left unturned. They explained it all and I felt like I was right there with them the whole way.

Steve would later say he was so exhausted that he had no idea what happened. And when I go back and watch the video now, he does look completely worn out and barely functioning. But I knew right then and there—this was the seminal moment of the trip. This was exactly why we were out here. This was the moment. This interview with Sue Endsley. And the hair stood up on the back of my neck, quite literally, when I realized all this could be traced straight back to Steve's bizarre, Rain Man–like obsession with Winchester, Illinois. Definitely, definitely had to get to Winchester. 'If you say 'Winchester' one more time I'm going to kill myself!' I'd thought. But none of this would've happened had we taken any other course.

How could he have known? He couldn't.

And that was the point.

CHAPTER 25

After hugs with Sue and Cindy in the parking lot, Rebecca graciously leaves us the keys to her church. "Do whatever you want. If you want to sleep inside, use the bathroom, whatever."

Usually I could find a small patch of grass somewhere to set up the orange bubble, but this lot was wall to wall concrete. Nothing. I have the keys to the church, so I decide to sleep in the room where we did the interview. The room was warm and inviting so I grab my sleeping bag and a pillow and climb back up the stairs. I plug my phone into a wall outlet and turn on a ball game.

I wiggle into my sleeping bag and it feels like I left Winchester a week ago. I can't believe it was this morning. A lot happened today, to say the least. The good, the bad and most certainly the ugly. Illinois truly felt like God's country and I was thankful. I'd live to fight another day and plan on riding 70 miles the next day to be in Mattoon, Illinois, by early afternoon.

The following day the forecast holds—it is another beautiful day. I should be resting all day to recover from yesterday's vertigo attack, but no, that wasn't going to happen. By riding less than 24 hours later, I'm flipping another middle finger to the Monster. At the beginning of this trip, I rode on adrenaline. Then I fought the insane heat and sun, only to turn around and endure freezing rain and hog trucks. Then I topped it all off with a full-blown vertigo attack.

I don't have much left in the tank, let's be honest, so I ride to Mattoon mostly on autopilot. I eat more bananas, apples, and peanut butter sandwiches. I also double my water intake. That morning as we discussed my route, we also decided I needed to take more breaks and sit in my chair more often.

At home I would be clocked out, in bed with the shades pulled down, recovering in the dark. On a good day at home I might get a load of dishes done, maybe clean the kitchen or vacuum the floor, but the day after an attack everything is off the table. It's in bed, in the dark, in the quiet of my safe place.

Riding 70 miles today is pure stupidity. But I need to see if I can do it. Dave stays closer than normal and so do Brian and Emmitt. If I can pull this off, I'll take tomorrow off and rest. And that's exactly what we do.

I roll into our destination in Mattoon, Illinois, in the early afternoon, right on schedule. The weather is still gorgeous, just as it has been all day. I reward myself with a visit to my favorite restaurant, Buffalo Wild Wings, for a tall beer and a 12 carton of hot wings. Thank you, Illinois, for sticking a B-dubs right across the street from our hotel.

We take the whole next day off to rest and it benefits us all. Brian hits a local laundromat, Dave works on social media, and I schedule a hair appointment. Yes, I got a haircut. In one hour, I go from Tom Hanks in *Castaway* to Kevin Bacon in *Murder in the First*.

Since I wear a hearing aid in my left ear, I either have to keep my hair very long or very short. When my hair is at a certain length, the hair pokes into the receiver and causes feedback and scratching noises. This was happening a lot now and I didn't want to wait for my hair to grow longer with everything else I was trying to focus on. So I chopped it.

My wife, Emily, normally cuts my hair and I haven't been to a barber in more than 20 years. Out here I have no choice. But it was worth it. I deal with enough insane ringing in my ear, so getting the hair out of my hearing aid was a good decision.

We're set to leave early the next morning and by day's end we should be in Indiana. Our target city is Terre Haute. Brian calls Cindy back in Taylorville and gets permission to crash at another Methodist Church. Like I said, 'God's country.'

I wake up feeling better from the previous day of rest. I've recovered fully from my attack and am ready to tackle the day. I make a short morning send-off video, flashing my new haircut and looking better than I have in days. The whole team rolls out—destination: Terre Haute. Once in Indiana we'll be one state away from Ohio, with Columbus only halfway through the state. I can't believe we are finally on the homestretch and I use every bit of that to motivate me rolling forward.

I walked into the office with a manilla folder stuffed under my arm. The folder contained all my medical records. It was two inches thick and held three years of collected medical data. My hopes were not high because no one had helped me so far. The bar was set low and I felt I was most likely chasing the wild goose once again. But my health was getting worse.

One day I was retrieving my son from his friend's house after a 12 hour video game marathon. The youngster's mother worked at our local hospital up in the mountains. She knew I'd been sick for a while and asked how I was doing.

"Not well," I told her. I explained my escalating symptoms and her eyes refocused.

"I have a friend going through similar things. She's seeing a doctor in Denver and likes him a lot. I could get his number for you if you want?"

"Sure," I said without skipping a beat, but still a hint of doubt in my voice.

Why not? This would be number ten. What have I got to lose? My vertigo attacks were increasing. They hit me three to four times a week now and my life was slipping away. I drove heavy equipment to support my family and as an accomplished musician I brought in some extra cash on the side. I'd been a bass player since the fourth grade and music was one of the loves of my life. Not anymore. All that was gone. I couldn't hear the notes correctly anymore, so

I gave it up years ago. I also couldn't be counted on to be a reliable employee anymore. I was having vertigo attacks while driving snow plows, and that's not the safest proposition, especially in the Rocky Mountains.

Everything I did and loved was a thing of the past.

Working menial jobs where I safely couldn't kill myself or injure someone had become my reality and this had the effect of crushing my self-esteem. My full-time job was now visiting specialists who couldn't seem to do anything for me.

So walking into this particular guy's office, the one recommended to me by the helpful mom, felt like just another futile attempt that would lead toward more dis-appointment. My mother used to tell me, "At least you have your health," a stupid cliche I always brushed aside as bullshit. It always seemed the dumbest thing I'd ever heard. Looking back now, I wish I would have been more grateful. Because I'm not getting my health back. The things I loved are things in the past from another life I took for granted.

Walking into this new doctor's office— that was my life now. Another doctor most likely with no answers and no help. I faced an unlivable life, with a future full of unanswered questions, combined with daily suffering that I never signed up for.

"At least you have your health . . . "

Indeed

PART 6

Indiana: The Hoosier State

Mattoon, Illinois-Terre Haute, Indiana, 63 miles
Terre Haute, Indiana-Indianapolis, Indiana, 83 miles
Indianapolis, Indiana-Knightstown, Indiana, 49 miles
Knightstown, Indiana-Richmond, Indiana, 44 miles

CHAPTER 26

September 18th, 2020

Day 18

Staying off the major highways isn't hard to do.

There are country roads criss-crossing all over middle America. The problem is navigating them. When Bill was with us, he and Dave were concerned about me constantly having to dig my phone out of my pocket while riding to check Google Maps, answer the phone, or change my music. Chances of dropping the phone was a real concern, but me crashing while distracted was an even bigger problem.

Back in St. Joe on our day off, Dave and Bill took my bike to get my back tire replaced. The tread had worn bare so this was a pre-emptive strike to stave off another flat. They left me to rest in the hotel room and ran to the bike shop and Walmart. The tire was fixed without a hitch, and at Walmart Bill found a phone mount that velcroed to my handlebars. It was a zippered case with a clear plastic cover so the touchscreen on the phone would work. Ingenious. And waterproof. It was perfect for me.

I am now basically hands free. No more digging around in my pocket. If my phone rings, I just reach down and hit a button, pull down my headset mic, and it works great. The other bonus is I can Google Map my route each day and see it easily on the screen with a quick downward glance. I can tell exactly where I am and where I am heading.

Leaving Mattoon, Illinois, and heading to Terre Haute, Indiana, my Google Maps is invaluable. I'll be changing roads so often that having a live map at a glance will make things much easier. The Google Lady's voice interrupts my music with a quiet ping and she says, "In 1,000 feet take a right on County Road 3355." Another quiet ping and it's back to Iron Maiden's 'Flight of Icarus.'

It all started as a beautiful relationship between me and the Google Lady. In my solitude and loneliness I began to have conversations with the computer voice. It was probably a slide toward clinical insanity, but I would thank Google Lady each time she led me in the right direction. Out loud, no less. Yes, insanity. But what could I do? Google Lady began to grow on me and I felt less lonely on the road. But like every relationship, there would be ups and downs.

Terre Haute is soon in my sights, but I need a battery switch just outside of town approximately 13 miles from our destination. I call Dave and he meets me at a roadside power station. It's a small, gravel parking lot with some sort of fenced-in bomb shelter looking building. We're nearly done for the day, but again I have to traverse a tricky bridge crossing.

Damn bridges. The roads are confusing, and my

route is in question.

In the shade of the van, I lean my head back in my chair and sigh. "What's the plan?" I ask Dave.

In the chair next to me, Dave says, "Brian's at the church and he's talking with a janitor or maintenance guy about the best and safest route."

I'm looking at Google Maps on my phone to survey my options when Brian calls. Brian talks to me with this maintenance guy's voice constantly chattering in the background. They're throwing different routes back and forth, and it becomes so confusing I've quickly had enough. I snap. Totally snap.

It has only been a 63 mile day, but I'm hot and frustrated. Being so close and not having a definite plan sends me over the edge. I hang up the phone mid-conversation. My irritability, another symptom of the Monster, has gotten the better of me. I know the team is doing their best to make this work, but there are a thousand moving parts to each day's journey. At that one moment in time, it all collapses in on me and I resort to what can only be described as a childish tantrum.

Dave, thankfully, sits in the other chair patiently while I scream a string of obscenities that'd make Bobby Knight's hair stand on end. I'm in a full-on, uncontrolled rage and to Dave's credit, he rides it out with a blank expression and no interference. He knows I'm not upset with him, or Brian, or anything to do with the trip. I just need to unload some stress. And that's what I do. In spades.

I slowly calm down and take a deep breath. I swallow some water and cram half a peanut butter sandwich down my gullet, if for no other reason than to shut myself up. I'm tired of hearing myself bitch.

"Okay," I say to Dave, much calmer now. "I heard both of them say I would have to go by the courthouse at some point, so let's start there."

Dave agrees. "I'll drive over the bridge, and if there's any issues, I'll give you a call. If you don't hear from me, you're all clear. I'll stop at the courthouse and wait for you there."

"Sounds good. I'll catch you there and we'll decide what's next."

In some ways it seemed we were making this harder than it needed to be, but we knew by then navigating bridges and getting through bigger cities was not something to take lightly.

After Dave fills my water bottles, I give him a head start to check things out and possibly call me back with his recon. In my lingering irritation, I think of Brian and Emmitt safely at the church and want to be there, right then, sitting in my chair with my day's ride comfortably behind me.

CHAPTER 27

Dave calls. I'm still sitting by the chain-link bomb shelter in the shade.

"So leading up to the bridge is not bad," he says, "but there's a lot of construction. The entire right lane is closed to traffic leading up to and across the bridge. The good news is I saw a person riding a bike in the closed lane. I think you can use that, too. It looks kind of confusing at first, but you'll understand when you get there."

"Ok," I reply, quite relieved.

"Once over the bridge, go straight for six blocks. I'm parked on the right side of the road across from the courthouse. You can't miss me."

Eager to get this day behind me, I take a last sip of water, snap on my ass bag and put my phone in its mobile home so I can see Google Maps.

With the bridge several miles away, I'm soon riding down Main Street into West Terre Haute. This is not the most prosperous section of town, to say the least. If you live here you're on the wrong side of the tracks, or in this case, the wrong side of the river that divides Terre Haute. Store fronts are boarded up more often than not. I pass liquor stores and check cashing operations, mixed with the occasional pawn shop. It's the buckle of the Rust Belt, but I actually enjoy the ride.

Like I said before, I love city life and feel like these are my people. I've always felt at home in places like this. I stop at a red light and a random dude on the corner waves me over. 'Okay,' I think. 'Time to mix it up with the locals.' Thoughts of my day's destination and the stress of finding the courthouse go out the window. My trip was about meeting people I would never meet in my 'normal' life, so I really want to meet this guy. I hop off my bike and push it to the curb.

"What are you riding there?" The guy points to my pink bike covered in stickers with sponsorships and other weird, assorted stuff I've slapped on during my trip (including decorative 'Day of the Dead' Mexican skulls).

"It's an E-bike," I reply.

"I wouldn't leave that sitting around this part of town if I were you," he says slyly.

"Well, I don't plan to," I tell him. "I'm just riding through town on my way to Columbus, Ohio."

"Wow, that's cool man," I get in return.

He's five foot nothing and stocky, probably in his early to mid 30's. He could give a fire hydrant a run for its money, and I like him instantly. He's full-on blue collar with his jeans and dirty clothing, just like me. I figure he just got off work and was walking home. Maybe he was in the construction trade or painting houses, I don't know.

But I am sure that he is wearing the coolest fuckin' old-school Hall and Oates t-shirt I've ever seen. For someone his age, a Hall and Oates shirt seems quite out of place. Back in my 'Blizzard of Oz' days of high school, to admit you'd even heard a Hall and Oates song, much less *liked* it, was grounds for an immediate ass kicking. But now, at 53 years old, I have to say I have a soft spot for Hall and Oates. I love their music, along with many other 80's pop sensations my 16-year-old self would kick my ass for admitting now.

This guy tells me his name is Josh and we talk about my trip and all I'd been through. He has a gentle spirit, but I sense his life has not been easy. At one point I say, "Man, I know this is a bit off topic, but that's the coolest Hall and Oates shirt I've ever seen."

"This old thing?" he says in surprise, waving me off like I was an idiot. "I found this in a cardboard box in a dumpster a couple months ago. Had like 30 old concert shirts in it. This was just the one I threw on this morning."

"I love it," I tell him.

We chat some more before parting ways and I tell him he's the coolest dude I've met since I left Denver. He immediately pulls the shirt off his back and offers it to me. "You can have this, man."

"I can't accept that," I back off, stammering. "That's too cool for you to give up."

He replies, "I really don't have any attachment to it. You seem to like it and I don't have anything to donate to your trip. I wish I did, but I don't. So please take it. It would make me happy."

How did I just become the luckiest man alive? And I don't mean that sarcastically, I really mean it.

I tell him, "Thank you, this means more to me than any amount of money you could give. You just gave me, quite literally, the shirt off your back." He looks at me with sad, compassionate eyes. Probably thought 'This guy's off his nut!' or something.

We end our exchange and he bids me good luck. "I hope you get to Columbus," and with that he turns and walks away in scuffed-up sneakers, paint splattered jeans, and buck naked from the waist up.

For a few seconds I'm stunned at the bizarre but awesome scene that just transpired, and stuff the shirt into the bag above my back fender. Before I roll, I double-check to make sure I zipped it up good and tight. (Out of laziness and brain fog, I'd already lost clothing due to my lack of concentration. Dave would sometimes find these on the side of the road and have to pick them up.) I feel like I've just been given the Shroud of Turin and I wasn't losing this shirt. I love inner-cities and meeting people like Josh. I wasn't worthy.

My spirits are now soaring high and it's back to the task at hand. Where is this construction Dave told me about?

I continue ten more blocks or so and see the flashing construction sign telling people to move over to the left lane. Let's see if Dave was right. Traffic is thick but I approach the construction and squeeze a gap between the orange barrels. Of course I get honked at by a car I cut off to enter the construction lane, but it's worth it and smooth sailing all the way across the bridge. I find the courthouse easily enough and Dave parked right where he said he'd be.

He looks a bit concerned at how long it took me to simply cross the bridge. "I wasn't sure whether to come back for you or what." I describe my encounter with Josh, and Dave also being a Hall and Oates fan in his old age, loves the story. We take pictures of me in the shirt in front of the courthouse till a local cop gets antsy and we decide to move along.

But the Hall and Oates shirt would become a huge part of the rest of our trip as we tried to squeeze it into every picture or video. We'd throw it on everyone (who'd allow us) so they'd have a picture with it, too. It was great fun and fodder for tons of laughs. And I guess if every great cause has to have its flag, then we'd just found ours.

CHAPTER 28

After meeting Josh and receiving his gift of the t-shirt, I gain a second wind. I didn't know Dave was filming me as we cruised through downtown Terre Haute, but I'm glad he did. Easily keeping up with traffic, I ride parallel to a semi-truck the whole way through the city. I chat with the man on the passenger side as we stoplight hop all the way through town. He's incredulous as to how I'm keeping up with them and I tell him about my E-bike. At the last light he waves me good luck and Dave gets the whole thing on video.

Besides the bike, my attire gives me away as an alien just passing through everywhere we go. I stand out like a sore thumb all the way across the Midwest and love every second of it. My outfit of white shirt, Iron maiden socks, bright riding vest, and black arm sleeves (peppered with skulls) opened up opportunities to talk about my trip. I'd made many friends along the way and the generosity I discovered in so many people gave me hope. Everywhere I went people were interested and attentive. I found it easy to tell my story. But this had been a long day and I was eager to find the church and rest.

I weave with the van through the city and Dave and I find ourselves on a rolling hill as we approach the church. My battery is about to die, so I wave Dave ahead and have to ride the last mile on muscle and willpower. I join Dave shortly at the church and it's another gem.

Brian had once again done a great job finding a wonderful place to stay for the night and again, the best part—it's free. This time we don't have access to the church facilities, but Brian's camper is up and running and we have everything we need. The maintenance guy did allow him to plug into an exterior outlet, so I start charging my batteries immediately. I walk around the side of the building and find a nice patch of grass to pitch my tent.

I'm not in the mood for our usual cold-cuts, cheese, and Gatorade, so we discuss dinner options. Being in a bigger city means more options and Emmitt Googles local eateries on his phone.

"KFC, Taco Bell, Chick-fil-A. Wait a second, Chick-fil-A!" Emmitt and Dave's eyes light up at that prospect. "It's only two miles away," Emmitt informs. I'm not a fan so what else is close? "There's a White Castle right next to it." Now MY eyes light up.

Now, I know what you're thinking: White Castle. That's the worst, most unhealthy crap you can put in your body. Especially when you're looking for pure protein and clean carbs. But to hell with it. Every once in a while I just need to indulge in something bad. The team looks at me sideways and I can read their minds: This guy's trying to kill himself. But whatever. To me I thought since I couldn't get White Castle in Colorado, here I was going to tempt fate, and indulge in a guilty pleasure.

It has been a tough day emotionally with lots of ups and downs but after Brian and I demolish a Crave-Case of White Castle rectum-rockets, I'm in a good mood. I'm even feeling up to playing some board games with the fellas in Mallory that night before hitting the orange bubble. I put on the Hall and Oates shirt as I climb into my sleeping bag and I feel like I'm the luckiest man alive.

Ménière's be damned.

I wake the next morning way before the team, as usual, and not wanting to wake Brian and Emmitt by entering the camper, I stack a grumpy in the woods behind the church. This also has become part of my routine, me pooping in a discreet location before the sun came up so as not to wake the team. Brian stumbles out with his obligatory Mountain Dew and helps strap on my gear and ready my bike for the day's ride.

Along with Dave, Brian's not an early bird and my schedule seems to be taking a toll on him, too. Emmitt, being in high school, never saw the light of day till noon or so, but that's what being a teenager is all about.

Last night, after my usual radio ball game, I wasn't able to sleep and I climbed out of the orange bubble and took my nightly stroll. Mallory was quiet and still, Brian and Emmitt were out cold. I passed Dave's van and could hear Hall and Oates greatest hits faintly seeping out. Dave was taking his Hall and Oates seriously. I liked that. Still wearing Josh's shirt, I smiled and was so glad to be with my brothers. The three of us were trying to do something special. Their sacrifice to help make this dream come true overwhelmed me and I couldn't appreciate them enough.

Once again I thought to myself, I'm the luckiest man alive.

Yesterday, during my endless hours on the bike I had called my father. He answered and instantly I heard the maps and papers unfolding. "Where're you heading now?" he asked.

"Brian found a church in Terre Haute for tonight, and he's there now. Tomorrow we want to get to Indy. What have you got?" He mentioned our cousin Mary Lynn, whom I hadn't seen in 30 years, lived there now, so maybe give her a call? At the very least, she could help with directions navigating the city.

"Okay, can you text me her number?"

With my new phone setup I dialed her on the roll and pulled my headset mic down when she answered,

"Hello."

"Hey! It's Steve, your cousin. My dad just told me you live in Indianapolis . . . " I couldn't help but picture the little 14-year-old that her brother and I used to pick on relentlessly, but she's married now to a great guy named Jim and they have a nice place on a lake in a west Indy suburb.

"Come here and stay. We'd love to have you guys!" she said enthusiastically.

Perfect.

"Great. Be there tomorrow afternoon."

I leave Terre Haute at the ass crack of dawn excited about the day's target: My cousin Mary Lynn's place 83 miles away. I can't wait to see her and catch up. It had been a really long time, but what I hadn't expected was that my long lost cousin had literally turned into one of the funniest people I'd ever have the pleasure to be around.

CHAPTER 29

How could you do this to me? I thought we had an understanding, a trust. And you went and betrayed my trust. I trusted you, Google Maps Lady, and you broke my heart! Did I not keep up my end of the bargain? You were to guide me safely through the twists and turns of the rural midwest, and in return I would thank you. That was our deal. . . Wasn't it? Well, after today our relationship is on thin ice, my dear. I don't know what I did to piss you off, but you didn't have to take it out on me the way you did.

After my vertigo attack we scaled my miles way back. For the rest of the trip I would never hit 100 miles in a day. We were ahead of schedule and reaching Terre Haute put me over the 1,100 mile mark. We still had a week left to hit our target date of September 25th and doing fewer miles a day just made sense. Today would be my last big push, 83 miles to be exact. It was more than I wanted to do, but we had a place in Indianapolis for the night and I was excited to see my cousin. Even though it was fewer miles than some of my bigger days, it turned out to be the longest day on my bike timewise, just over 12 hours.

It wasn't the weather, or my health, that slowed me down. No, it was Google Maps. On any given map, Route 40 ran straight between point A and point B of the day's destinations. But Route 40 was big and heavily trafficked and I wasn't sure about shoulder room for my bike. Last night during our camper chill time we decided a back roads route slightly north of 40 looked best, and we plotted it out. North to Greencastle, switch batteries. East to Coatesville, switch batteries again, then safely on to Indy. But I only made it as far as Carbon on the first battery. And here's why.

I'm up early this morning and it's cold out. I layer up and the team and I make a morning send off video as we shiver in the back parking lot of the church. I would be doing a mere 83 miles, but want to get a jump on it. I want to make sure to arrive at my cousin's house before rush hour in Indy. As a city of just under one million, this was by far my most intimidating destination.

I lived in Indianapolis from ages 3-7 and the last time I rode a bike there, it was a Big Wheel on my driveway on 106th St. This trip, I'd have an opportunity to ride straight through the center of a major metropolis and I couldn't wait. But first thing's first. I had to reach today's destination safely with as much energy preserved as possible and no vertigo attacks. A tall order indeed.

I'm soon shedding layers as the sun starts its day. By now I have my shedding routine down to a science and always leave extra space in the rack bag. By the end of most days, I felt like I was carrying a rugby ball strapped to my fender. It wasn't super comfortable or efficient, and it looked ridiculous. The ass bag around my waist also holds the day's odds and ends, such as my winter cap and toilet paper.

I carried toilet paper, everyday and everywhere, without fail. You never knew when nature would call for a squat in a cornfield to squeeze out my personal brand of fertilizer. You're welcome, farmers of America. Glad I could help. On this day I doubled my dose of TP in case last night's run-in (no pun intended) with White Castle came back to haunt me. It didn't. Sometimes I think God even smiles on the idiotic. And those with bowels full of White Castles.

Anyway, I was doing really well for the first five miles, but alas, this wouldn't hold. It happened when Google Maps Lady, my best friend now, decided to betray

191

me. It would be our first argument, but not our last.

Ping! "In 2,000 feet go left on County Road, blah, blah." My road was obviously coming to a dead end and my only option was to go left, but I said out loud anyway, "Thank you, Google Lady." I wanted her to know I appreciated her attentiveness, even if I only had one choice. That's how our relationship worked thus far. But this time, I made the left and found myself smack in the middle of nowhere.

The guys back at the church are barely starting their day, so it's up to me to get myself to the first stop. I slow down, not voluntarily as a precaution in my bewilderment, but because I am sinking into six inches of gravel. I don't mind riding gravel roads, I'd been on a few already. A hard-packed gravel road took extra concentration, but it was doable. This is *not* a hard-packed gravel road. It's loose and deep and equivalent to riding in a foot of mud.

After I make the turn, and almost lose my balance, my music pings off and I get my next set of instructions. Google Lady says in my ear, "Stay on County Road something or other for six miles." What the hell, Google Lady? Six miles of riding this shit? I don't think so.

My bike suddenly shimmies hard and I downshift quickly to avoid spinning out. I can barely keep my bike upright as it sloshes side to side as I try to peddle in this shit. Oh, that my biggest problem was the possibility of an ass explosion from greasy fast food at this point. I had enough butt wipe to handle *that* problem. But now, on the gravel, I'm in serious trouble. Hopefully it'd only be a short stretch under repair and I'd soon be on normal road again. Wrong! Loose, sloshy gravel for the *entire* six miles.

I'm exhausted after half a mile and come to a halt. Fuck this. I double check my phone to see if there was an earlier turn off I missed. Nope. How about a quick turn-off ahead onto a better road? Nope again. Fuck.

I usually average 18-20 mph in good weather and solid roads. Now I can barely keep up 5 mph. This was going to be a long and excruciating ride. I'm only one hour into my day and I'm fighting the bike, fighting discouragement and sweating like a dog. My legs are churning like a paddle boat on crack and it takes me more than an hour to finish that six mile death strip. Fuck you, gravel road, and fuck you, Google Bitch! Now, for the record I don't use this derogatory term towards women. So y'all don't get your panties in a wad. If it was a man's voice giving directions that ruined my day, I'd probably call him Google Dick or something like that.

Contemplating all these things, my phone pings. "In 1,000 feet turn left on County Road whatever." Knowing I'm approaching my turn lightens my mood. Just kidding, it did not. I am pissed, exhausted, tired, and sweating like Ned Beaty's pig. I'm 11 miles into an 83 mile day and it hits me, 'This is going to be a long, very long day.' Not to mention the drain it is putting on my battery.

I finally reach my turn and go left. Ping! "Stay on County Road what the fuck for four miles." It's a dirt driveway leading to a grain silo. What am I supposed to do with that? The silo is 50 feet tall and the only structure within miles. I cruise the dirt driveway and dead end into a fence surrounding the silo.

This can't be right.

CHAPTER 30

What the hell is going on? Why is Google Lady, now Google Bitch, suddenly hating me so much? What had I done to her to deserve such crass and brutal behavior? I'm not on any kind of road at all and it dead ends into a grain silo. I'm jumbled and exhausted from miles of gravel torture and then, lucky me, that's when my brain fog kicks in. When this happens, I can't focus. On anything.

Under the stress and anxiety of it all, not to mention what the day still held, I collapse like a heap of shit on a dirt pile. Me being a heap of shit—figurative, the dirt pile—real. I need to get my shit together, and fast. I need to hydrate and have some jerky and a sandwich.

After 15 minutes I decide to double check my phone for directions. The green line on my map says I'm right where I'm supposed to be. Supposedly, the road is just past the silo I'm sitting next to. Okay, I think, if I push my bike around the fence enclosing the silo I'm sure to find a nice country road that keeps me on course. Yeah, it was a rutted out ATV trail. Shit! But my phone confirms this is it. And it's my only option.

For the love of God!

The road, if you can call it that, is so rutted nothing is flat. This was where good ole boy high schoolers came for a good time after a downpour to muddy the shit out of their trucks so they could look cool when they pulled up to the high school Monday morning. I know how it is because I also went mudding in my four wheel drive truck back in the day. And I thought I looked pretty cool driving around like that. "That dude is hardcore!" But I am not in a truck. I am not even on an ATV. I am on a fucking bicycle out in the middle of nowhere. I am stuck.

Not literally, but figuratively.

The thought of turning around to backpedal six miles of Satan's ass crack makes me want to throw up. Literally, not figuratively. I couldn't do it again even if I wanted, so I resign myself to fate. If Google Maps Lady—my darling turned Lex Luther—decided to send me this way, then so be it. I climb back on my bike and begin riding again. But I am not happy about it. My bike bumps and jumps over the rugged dirt ruts. The thought I could actually get tossed off and break my neck (or back) floats across my brain as I grip the handlebars tighter.

After a mile of feeling like a human paint-mixer, the road, if you could call it that, meanders into a river bed. A river bed! I am now riding on sand. On a 60 pound bike. Dried, fallen tree branches and scrubs litter the bed.

What the fuck am I doing?

And that's when I hear it like the sound of angels belting out the hallelujah chorus: Traffic noise. I glance at my phone, which to my surprise is still working after the sheer punishment it's taking on, and realize I'm going to intersect I-70 around the next bend. I bask in the sounds of civilization but I can't ride on I-70. It isn't legal.

My river bed takes me under the freeway overpass. I couldn't get up there even if I wanted to. There is no way to push my bike up the steep embankments. So I carry on.

Soon I come upon four packed dirt barriers. Spaced one hundred yards apart, they were probably put there by heavy equipment operators to keep shitheads like me from traveling down this insane road. Well, shitheads in cars or trucks, let's say. 'But,' I scream in my head, 'this isn't a road, it's a fucking riverbed!' I stop and look around once more at my absurd situation that has quickly taken a steep plunge into deeper absurdity. But I have no choice.

I drag my super heavy E-bike up and over the first eight foot high, packed dirt roadblock. I do this four times. I have no other choice. After hauling my bike the fourth time over Lucifer's testicles, I serpentine weave twice more under I-70 for another two miles. Fuck!

Ping! "In 1,000 feet turn right."

One thousand feet reveals a service road that parallels the freeway. I stop on the blacktop and feel like kissing the pavement like an Apollo 13 astronaut. But instead I park my bike for a sip of water and spend five minutes checking the bike for possible issues. I've just given it the beating of its life and need to know if there was any permanent damage.

I call Dave and explain what happened and he meets me soon after at a truck stop to switch batteries. He tells me the boys were way up ahead in Coatesville, waiting.

I leave the truck stop and head across an overpass that carries me over I-70. After the morning's debacle, I'm completely spent. I'm not even halfway to Indy and I feel like I've ridden more than 300 miles already.

My brain fog is kicking my ass and I have to trust Google Bitch to get me to Coatesville with no more shenanigans.

The rural road she puts me on this time is fantastic. Two lanes, lined with trees, good pavement, and rolling hills. I look down at my speedometer to see I'm cruising at an easy 25 mph. After the morning's slugfest, I feel like I'm going to break the sound barrier.

Dave catches up with Brian and Emmitt in Coatesville and they find a community center that allows them to charge the spare battery. It'll never charge in time in the van, and we are in the middle of a huge day. In the meantime I'm completely zoned out. I'm making good time and could maybe make up for my slow and discouraging start.

The good pavement feels great and my mind floats to thoughts of seeing my cousin in Indianapolis and relaxing. I pass quaint, country homes every four hundred yards or so. It's peaceful and pretty. I begin to finally relax on the bike. I meander tree-lined bends where the road gently rises up and back down, again and again. There's no traffic and I have the road to myself.

Something in the corner of my eye catches my attention. Fifty feet behind me, a Doberman pinscher has given chase. At me! Shit! Hauling ass at full speed, he'll be on me in seconds. I pray he's near his house and trained to stop and return out of loyalty and discipline.

Nope.

Not a fuckin' chance. He keeps coming, quickly closing the gap.

I gear up into Turbo, a bike setting I only use in extreme cases. Turbo sucks the battery like nobody's business but this is no time to worry about losing juice. This is an all-out competition for speed, and my life is on the line. Where's his goddamn owner? Somebody call him off! I glance in my rear-view and Cujo is nearly upon me. Jesus! How fast can he go?

One thing is for sure at that point, nobody is going to call him off. I glance down and my speedometer reads 29.5 mph as he pulls alongside. His teeth are bared and sharp and his eyes glare at me like I'm a hot dog on opening day at Fenway. If there was ever a time I was going to explode White Castles all over God's green earth, it was now. I kick at him a couple times but this only works to slow me down.

I decide to pedal him into the ground in the race of his life. We'd easily covered more than two hundred yards by now, and even a cheetah runs out of juice eventually, right? At 300 yards he is spent. I see him slow down in my mirror, and he comes to a complete stop. Whew, damn. What the hell? Could this day get any crazier?

By now the boys are all happily in Coatesville awaiting my arrival. Brian calls and tells me how to find a nearby bike path, which gives me a smooth, traffic free cruise into town.

Unbeknownst to me, Brian has grabbed Dave's bike and come back to meet me. It's noon and I'm not even halfway to Indianapolis. My daily frustrations are getting the better of me and my anxiety is skyrocketing. I see Brian stop on the trail facing me with the GoPro on his head. I ride straight into his face and gamble that the film is rolling. I rant into the camera for 60 seconds about how much Google Bitch had let me down and who knew a goddamn Doberman could run 30 mph?

I calm down, the stress off my chest, and we stop not long after to chat with a group of enthusiastic mountain bikers riding to raise awareness for the completion of the bike path we are on. They describe their cause and I describe mine in turn, and two of them hand me a donation for my ride. I'm taken aback at their generosity, and to this day I wish them the very best. And good luck to them with the bike trail. The part I was on was awesome.

Just to add to the shit show of the day, shortly thereafter Brian blows a tire. After all I'd been through, I don't have the energy to walk the two miles with him back to the community center. So, being the selfish ass that I am, I tell him good luck and start pedaling. I want this day to be done and being a good older brother is at the bottom of my list.

CHAPTER 31

Twelve hours after leaving Terre Haute I arrive in west Indianapolis. (By the way, I did not beat rush hour. I hit it head on.)

It is great getting reacquainted with my cousin Mary Lynn, but I am wiped out. The truth about Ménière's or any invisible illness isn't that we look sick, it's the energy spent on acting not sick. It's exhausting to act healthy when you're not. Just saying.

We sit on her back porch under an awning and catch up. Thirty years has gone by. I barely even know her. I am sitting in a high-back lounge chair resting my head back and beginning to feel a bit more human. Truth be told, I am feeling so bad I want to crawl under a rock and die.

Mary Lynn's husband Jim whips up an awesome pulled-pork dinner and takes (non-Ménière's team members) on a pontoon tour of the lake behind the house. My cousin and I stay back and continue to laugh about old times. She is so funny and quick-witted, I ask her to help me with the end of day social media update.

I never script my update videos; Dave always starts filming and I shoot from the hip. Not too much goes into it except saying it's cold this morning and I'm going to ride 100 miles. One take and done, then Dave posts it, simple as that.

I lean on the pontoon tied to the dock, and with Mary Lynn standing beside me, Dave calls, "Action!" The problem is every time we start the video, we crack up. Take after take, and we can't stop laughing. It gets to the point we are all in tears. But I really need the humor after the day I had with the gravel, river bed and the Doberman. I am just grateful to be with family and friends.

Our visit with my cousin has been too short and on the way out in morning I tell her, "Let's not let another 30 years go by before we see each other again." She agrees and we leave her house excited that in five short miles our route would take us straight through one of sports' great cathedrals—the Indianapolis Motor Speedway. The sheer history of that place is unparalleled in racing and I can't wait to see it. Of course, us being Schwiers, we HAVE to figure out a way to get me on the track for a video.

Brian arrived before us and sweet-talked his way past the security guard at the entrance. The guy said there was a BMW exhibition race on the track, so we couldn't get on there, but he let us in the infield and gave us the run of the place. Holy crap! We are OK with that and make a silly video about me racing my bike, complete with a pit stop using Mallory, and it turns out awesome.

It was a total blast, people online loved it, and the weather was a perfect midwestern autumn day. Win-win-win!

Now it's off to try and get me through downtown Indianapolis. We plot a route straight through the heart of the city. I'm excited and more than a little nervous. We plan to rendezvous in a parking lot next to the bridge that would shoot me straight through downtown. I tell Dave I want to document the whole thing, so for the first time I strap the GoPro on my head.

Two bald eagles glide overhead, silent and majestic, floating over the river I would soon cross. It's an odd site with a metropolitan backdrop but I take it as a good omen.

I had decided on a 49 mile day that day, because:

#1-Yesterday kicked my ass.

#2-We spent a lot of time at the racetrack that morning.

#3-After my vertigo attack, I had decided to work less and rest more.

Knightstown, Indiana, would be our target today, but first I have to get through downtown Indianapolis. It is September 20th, my wife's birthday. I miss her and haven't seen her since day one of my trip. I will think about her often today.

I was hoping Sunday morning would again mean less traffic, and yes, the streets are mostly empty.

Many American cities are catching up with the times and becoming more bike friendly. Indianapolis is a great example. Since the bridge has a bike lane, this is my first stress-free bridge crossing of the trip. The bike lane goes all the way through downtown and into the eastern suburbs. I enjoy every second of it.

The symptoms I had battled so hard the day before were forgotten. This is what I call a 'good' day. Sure, my ear is ringing off the charts as always, but my dizziness, nausea, and fatigue are at a minimum, Thank God.

The team stays back until I call and say I'm doing well. Then they pass me somewhere downtown. Brian and Emmitt first, then Dave rides up a few minutes later, flashers on, and I give him the obligatory thumbs up. If I play my cards right, I won't need a battery change at all today and can simply meet them all in Knightstown, Indiana. I pass through the lower east side of Indy enjoying the joggers, dog walkers and Sunday morning churchgoers. You don't see humanity like this when you spend eight hours in the cornfields. I'm relaxed and in my element.

In an east side suburb, I need help finding the interchange that will take me on to Knightstown. I glance down at Google Maps and realize this could be a little tricky. I arrive at a roundabout, 100 feet in diameter, but with eight streets feeding into it. I turn right and start my loop.

Ping! "Take a left on Elizabeth Street."

What the fuck? A left? The center island on my left is a small park with trees and a couple of park benches. "There is no left," I tell Google Bitch out loud, and I see no Elizabeth Street. I go around the circle three more times, no idea where to turn.

Ping! "Take a left on Elizabeth Street."

Jesus Christ. I'm soon totally disoriented in my directions and nothing makes sense. I decide to pull into the middle of the circle and restart my phone.

Now, you have to understand, I've gotten on and off my bike hundreds of times this trip. It was something a five-year-old could do without thinking. But when I rolled to a stop near the benches, I thought I'd put my foot down. I really did. Turns out I hadn't. I topple over and hit the ground hard. I'm not even moving at the time. I just fell over.

My brain fog had erased what I was thinking and I forgot what I'd planned to do, which was to put my foot down. Simple as that. Already bruised and battered, when I fell the GoPro slammed down my forehead and hit me in the nose. 'Thank God I was wearing this,' I think as I reach to readjust it. 'This will be hilarious to have on video.'

And it was.

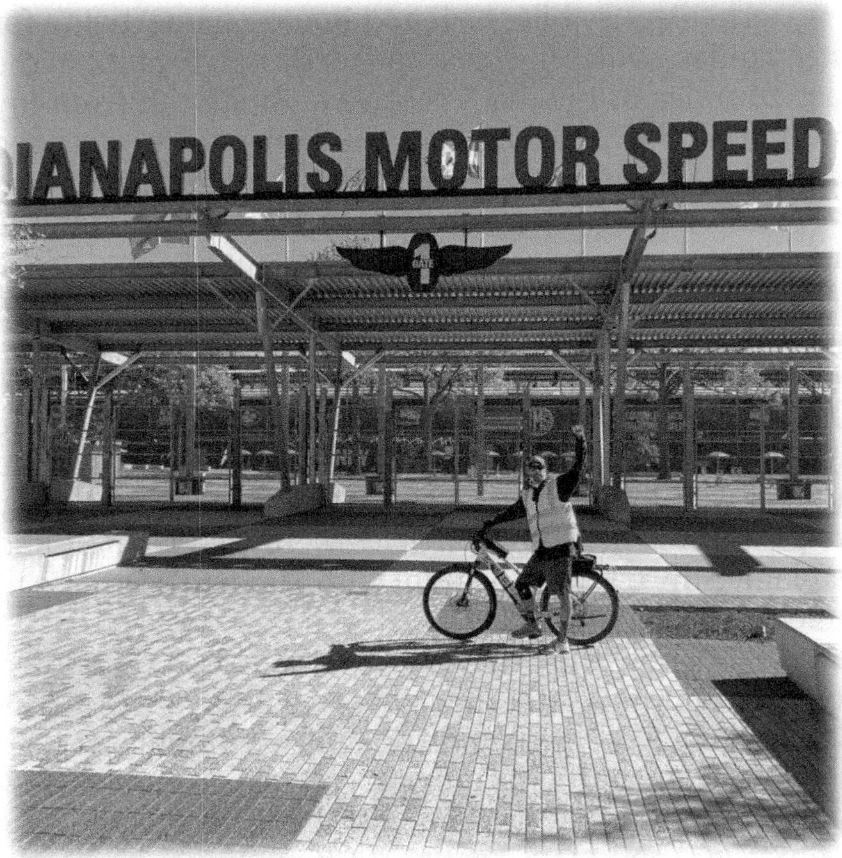
DIANAPOLIS MOTOR SPEED

After rebooting my phone I bring up my rebooted Google Maps. I never do find Elizabeth Street. But when I re-enter my destination I'm led to a sliver of bike path called the Pennsy Trail. This takes me straight through the suburbs and eventually most of the way to Knightstown.

The Pennsy bike trail and Route 40 intertwine for many miles, switching back and forth. At one point in the last 20 miles of my day I receive a phone call from my brother-in-law, Garth, back in Denver. He attended Otterbein University in Westerville, and upon graduating worked for local newspapers in the Columbus area. He lives in Denver now but still has contacts and close friends in Columbus. He was a great support to the trip and even went so far as to get me an interview with my hometown newspaper before we started. "Westerville Graduate on Journey Fighting Disease" read the headline and it came out the week before I left Denver. I was also interviewed by my local newspaper, *The Summit Daily News*, before I left. Both articles were well written and explained my trip and my fight with Ménière's Disease in precise layman's terms.

Somehow the article in Columbus was forwarded to the mayor of Westerville. Subsequently, Mayor Kathy Cocuzzi made some inquiries and eventually tracked down Garth as the originator of the article. "Hey, Steven," Garth says into my headphones. He still calls me 'Steven' and I love that about him. "I received a call from Mayor Cocuzzi and she wants to meet you at the finish line."

"Wow!" I reply. At that point in my trip, I'd planned for the finish line to be my father's front door in Westerville, Ohio. My father's house would involve little fanfare, and besides, I was just hoping to get there in one piece.

"Can I give her your contact info? She wants to talk to you," Garth says.

"Sure," I tell him.

Mayor Cocuzzi found out my timing was going to put me in Westerville on Friday, Sept. 25th. She would call a couple days later to discuss my homecoming; she is excited to meet me and would love to honor me on behalf of my hometown. We talk logistics and decide I would ride into Westerville and finish my ride at town hall. My father lives a few blocks from there so what the hell, why not? It seems like a fitting finish, but it's also a bit overwhelming.

My original plan was when (if) I made it to Columbus, I would quietly pull up to my father's doorstep, park my bike, and go inside and take a nap. Being received by the mayor of Westerville would kick my finish up a notch and sounded exhausting. But I felt grateful for the mayor's generosity, and also for the publicity it would give my ride. Not to mention, I'd be meeting a mayor! A public official was going to go out of her way to meet me after this crazy ass trip I'd thrown together in two months prior to leaving Denver, and after having done nothing but lie on the couch for years! What the hell? When did this become my life?

Dave:

You have to understand that a mere two and a half months earlier we were sitting on my nephew's porch after Steve had pitched this cockamamie idea, trying to decide if he was completely nuts, organizing a subconcious suicide mission, and/or grossly underestimating what it would take to pull

207

this off.

He was years on the couch! The most exercise he'd done was walk the dog each day around the park! And now he was going to ride a bike 1400 miles across America? This was crazy . . . pure madness.

Three days before we left Denver, I made a video expressing (in a comical way) how nervous I was with three days to go. Truth is, I was almost sick with nerves. What were we doing? This could've been the biggest disaster in the world and we were heading straight into it full speed! Were we careless or just plain dumb? But the other truth was that I never dwelled on catastrophic outcomes. We were going to make a plan, stick to it, and do everything we could to complete the journey. Even if it killed us. And it might.

Though we got the logistics of the trip working pretty quickly after leaving Denver, I would never have guessed in a million years how over the top successful the trip was to become. No idea. We raised far more money than I ever could've imagined. We met more people who were kind and incredibly generous than I ever could've imagined. We laughed harder and suffered more than I ever could've imagined. And best of all, I never, ever could've imagined how much this trip would mean to suffering folks in the Ménière's community.

And now we were also, on our arrival in Columbus, going to meet the Mayor of our hometown! It felt completely surreal. At that point the trip had gone so far into unseen outer dimensions that I was like, 'Meet the Mayor? Well, of course we are!' And I was jacked. Super excited for what that meant for Steve and the Ménière's community. After all, could there have been a higher validation that we, in fact, weren't crazy or completely bat-shit fucking stupid for doing this trip in the first place? Meeting the mayor was going to be the perfect cap to our over the top successful trip.

Yet one thing still concerned me. How would we get

Steve through this whole finishing process alive?

I arrive at the eastern edge of Knightstown at 4 p.m. Brian, Emmitt and Dave had parked behind a random church in the middle of town, but were having a hard time contacting anyone who could give us permission to stay there for the night.

We had run our 'actual' church contacts thin, and were just riding the wire at that point hoping for another miracle. Brian called the number on the info board out front, but was getting no answer. I later found out Brian and Emmitt had spent all afternoon dragging Mallory from one town to another, from one church to another, over seven in all, with no luck. Brian was waiting for a call back from a church camp two towns past Knightstown, but it didn't seem promising.

Dave had scouted Knightstown and planted himself behind a church just off the main drag. "This looks like our best bet if your church camp deal falls through," Dave told Brian. "There are three churches on this block. We'll keep trying them all while we wait for your person to call back."

"I know where you're at," Brian told him. "We're on our way."

Dave:

This was a bit worrisome. It was getting late in the afternoon and we hadn't secured permission to stay anywhere. We were in small town rural Indiana—it wasn't like a Motel 6 was just down the road. And in a small town, there was no getting away with just parking anywhere overnight. So Brian and I trotted around to several churches to no avail.

Not a human in sight. And this was a Sunday. It made no sense to me. Other towns had bustling church Sundays, even during this Covid pandemic. But all of a sudden . . . nothing.

After some more time of fruitless searching, Brian and Emmitt declared they were really hungry. "We haven't eaten all day."

"Ok," I told them as we walked a few blocks to the main street. "There's a Subway down there." I looked at Emmitt. His eyes lit up. He loves Subway.

"Great, let's go!" Brian chirped.

Carrying our subs back across town to the camper, we passed an odd mural of a coach with some basketball players. I stopped to gawk at it. So out of place. "Oh, yeah," Brian said, "we forgot to tell you, but this would be Steve and Dad's favorite town."

"Huh?"

"Well, the Hoosiers *gym is here. From the movie."*

Hoosiers *is one of our father's favorite movies of all time, if not his very favorite. I loved the movie too, and have seen it many times. Steve, being a very sporty dude, as all of us in our family are, loves all sports movies. Even the ones you've never heard of.*

I looked at Brian. "What are you talking about?"

"Earlier Emmitt and I were scouting the other side of town and we passed something that looked like a church. Emmitt ran up and it said 'Hoosier's Gym'."

"What?" I still wasn't comprehending.

My first thought was that it was the actual school gym where the real Hoosiers championship team was from. But that didn't seem right because I once looked it up and thought it was further south and east of where we were. "I gotta see this." I left Brian and Emmitt at the camper to eat their subs and took off across town.

Some bored local kids in the town square noticed an 'out of towner' hoofing his way somewhere in a hurry. "Hey, man, where are you going?" and they gave me some other teen crap trying to impress their friends. I ignored them. At the end of the long street I hurried down, I came to a small building with a plaque: "Hoosier's Gym."

'Huh,' I thought. 'Brian was right. From the outside it does kind of look like a church.'

A nice man met me inside the door and immediately introduced himself. I looked around. A trophy case on one wall, some black and white team photos of basketball players, a large screen TV playing the movie Hoosiers on a loop—yep, definitely the right place. "Is this where the team from Hoosiers was from?" I asked the nice man.

"No, this is where the movie was made." Just then I spotted a picture of Gene Hackman standing as 'coach' behind his team from the movie. I was slowly putting two and two together.

"So this is the actual gym . . . where it was filmed?"

"That's right."

He walked me through a door that smacked me like a ton of bricks. Not the door, but the scene. Even if you'd seen the movie once, you'd recognize it immediately. It was the Hoosiers gym, by God, straight from the celluloid.

'Holy shit!' I nearly said out loud, which probably would've been bad manners in front of such a nice, midwestern man. It never occurred to me that the movie wasn't filmed on a soundstage in Hollywood. I mean, how hard could it be to replicate a 1950's high school gymnasium? But they hadn't. They did it here . . . right where I was standing.

Again, you have to understand, we'd been doing 80s film parodies all across the country. And now here was an actual movie set . . . an honest to God real movie set. (I silently hoped the movie was from the 80s. Turns out it was—1986. Bam!) My next thought was, 'Steve and Dad are going to shit themselves when they find out . . . '

I called my dad immediately and told him where I was. My dad played high school basketball and still referees city leagues in Westerville, Ohio. He'd give any regular sports fan a run for their money. He told me, "Oh, my mother was friends with Bobby Plump's mother. I met him once when I was little, but my mother knew Bobby and his mother real well." Bobby was the real-life kid who made the winning shot in the state championship, immortalized in the movie.

I looked at the man next to me. It was obvious he was a volunteer and super committed to this whole scene. I handed my phone to the guy, "You might want to hear this." And I watched as my dad and a complete stranger bonded like eight-year-olds over this bit of coincidental history we'd just stumbled into. Even I didn't know my dad was that connected to the movie Hoosiers. No wonder he loved it so much.

The man finally hung up with my dad and said, "Do you want to see the locker room?"

And I was like, "You mean the locker room is here too?" I was like a kid in a candy store.

"Yeah, sure. Where the coach gave all the speeches in the movie." And he guided me across the gym.

He opened a gate and we went down the stairs, and sure enough, I knew it immediately. This was the exact locker room from the movie. I was starstruck by my surroundings. The tour guy plopped down on a bench by the door and said, "This is where Gene Hackman sat." And he recited several lines from the movie.

Holy shit. We were going to be able to reenact a movie scene at an actual movie set for social media! I was so excited I could've crapped myself. And that's when my phone rang.

My battery dies at the newly built Knightstown High School on the outskirts of town. I'm five miles shy of Dave and Brian, and figure the boys are waiting for me. I call Dave and give him my location. Then I lay under a tree in the shade to wait.

Dave:

"I'll come and get you. No problem." I knew I was going to send Brian because I wanted to make this a surprise. The Hoosiers *building closed at 5 p.m. and it was 4:40.*

I called Brian. "Steve's at the high school. He'll probably want to argue with you, but throw his bike in the van and get him here, quick!"

I'm counting the minutes to Dave bringing me a fresh battery. Five lousy miles, but that's a lot of work with no battery. I sit back and realize I'm really in no big hurry. I'm enjoying lying in the grass under a tree. The weather is perfect.

The van pulls up and Brian hops out, not Dave. "Throw your bike in the van, we need to go now." I hated to backtrack. It was only five miles to the church where they parked. I don't want to have to load my bike in the van tomorrow morning and drive back to the high school for God's sake.

But . . .

Brian has a sense of urgency that's confusing and a bit alarming. "Put your bike in the van. Emmitt's in the back. He'll watch it."

I stand still. My concern grows deeper. Dave usually shows up in the van. Why are Brian and Emmitt in the van? Where is Mallory, and more importantly, where is Dave? Oh shit, did something happen to Dave? 'Today has been a great day so far, please don't go south on me now!' I'm a little irritated, but a lot more worried.

"Tell me what's going on, Brian," I push.

"Dave's okay, he's in town. We stumbled upon the gym where they filmed *Hoosiers*. Dave is there now but it closes in 15 minutes. So we need to hurry."

Dave's where?

This comes so far out of left field I'm having a hard time wrapping my head around it. We load my bike and Brian drives the five miles in record time, with Emmitt in the back holding on for dear life.

As we pull up to the front of the gymnasium, my heart starts racing. I know it immediately. I've watched *Hoosiers* more times than I can count, and it was just like being thrown inside the movie.

It looks exactly like it should and I know it's going to be awesome.

CHAPTER 33

I'm a sports fanatic and love all sports movies. Any sports movies, it doesn't matter. But especially if it's done well. *Hoosiers* is one of the best, about an underdog small town high school basketball team that wins the Indiana state championship against all odds. It's freakin' brilliant. I own the DVD. It was actually sitting next to my DVD player back home right then.

Dave knew me well and asked the tour guy if we could shoot hoops in the gym. Yes, that's what I said, shoot hoops in the gym. *The gym.* For most of you out there, this may seem a bit unimportant, even nerdy. But we were in for an unforgettable experience, and it didn't disappoint.

My first few shots clank against the iron. BRICK! Then a few air balls. Then the sweet swish of nothing but net. In the *Hoosiers* gym, no less. If only my dad could see me now. The clock hits 5:00 and I look at the tour guy. Not only can he read my mind, but he's enjoying every second of seeing us out of towners completely geek out.

"Can we stay a bit longer?"

"Sure!"

Dave:

We shot hoops for a while, then I gathered everyone to show them the locker room. I was super excited. I knew they would appreciate it as much as I did. But more than that, I wanted to shoot the Gene Hackman scene where he's pissed at the team.

"This will be great!" I told Steve and Brian as they looked around. The tour guy was on hand to feed us lines. He had the whole movie memorized, of course.

"What's the scene again?" Steve asked. We told him, and he and Brian looked less than enthused. I don't think they thought the scene would be recognizable.

"You could do 'Welcome to Indiana basketball'," the tour guy offered. "That's a very famous scene."

So we went to the top of the stairs and Steve and I blocked the scene where Gene Hackman straightens his tie, sighs, looks up, says, "Welcome to Indiana basketball," and pushes the door open revealing a gym in full pre-game mode.

It's great.

So Steve does it, opening the door to Emmitt and Brian and the tour guy shooting hoops in the near court.

Hilarious.

I was super jacked and loved the short, but sweet, reenactment. It captured the movie perfectly.

So the only lingering issue from the day is that we still haven't locked down a place for the night. It's going on 6 p.m. and usually we'd be set up and relaxing by now, orange bubble and all.

We ask the curator if he knows anyone from the church where the camper was parked so we could get permission for the night. He does not. But a woman in the back office overhears our conversation and yells out to the lobby, "Why don't we give Bob a call?"

"It wouldn't hurt," the tour guy says.

In a few minutes the woman walks out. "Bob said he'd love to host you for the night."

Turns out not only was Bob also a volunteer at the gym, but he played on the team in 1966 that was last to use the gym for actual high school basketball. Not only that, he wrote a book about the movie called *Eleven Life Lessons* by Robert Garner. We also found out that years earlier Bob had ridden a bicycle cross-country on his own fundraiser for a chronic illness his wife had. She died shortly thereafter, but he was still an avid cyclist.

Apparently we have a lot in common.

We get directions to his place and it turns out he lives right across the street from the new high school where Brian had picked me up. Perfect. Now I wouldn't have to backtrack in the morning. Bob lives in a small apartment behind an auto garage that houses ambulances for the local EMTs. Behind the place is a huge concrete parking lot with a bunch of cars and not much else around. And it's free. So it's perfect for us.

Bob comes out and meets us shortly after set-up. We exchange stories and find out he has plenty of grandchildren. Dave writes middle-grade books for kids, the *Ayla Bayla* series, so after Bob passes each of us a copy of his book, Dave gives him a set of *Ayla Bayla* books for his grandchildren.

Then we all share a drink of whiskey and Bob suggests a great steakhouse in town. We are famished from our *Hoosiers* excitement and load into the van, leaving Bob to his quiet life.

Our waitress this evening is Charlie, fresh out of high school and a total smart ass (in the very best way possible). She's sassy to a fault and has us laughing all the way through dinner. We love her immediately. At one point she explains she knew a boy in high school who'd had a vertigo attack right in the middle of one of her classes.

"And the teacher didn't know what was happening, so she was pretty uncool about it. But *I* knew. I think I was one of the only people he ever told he had Ménière's."

She understood. This random out-of-the-blue waitress knows something about what I face each day. I appreciate her honest demeanor and we take some pictures out front before we leave. A great night and great day overall.

Back at Bob's there's no grass to be found, so I pitch the orange bubble right there on the concrete between Mallory and the van and I sleep like a baby. Leaving Indy that morning, again, feels like it was a week ago. A lot happened and I was very thankful. A rare day indeed, and I enjoyed it to the fullest. Tomorrow I'll be off to Richmond, Indiana, on the border of Ohio. This is the very first time I feel like we just might make it to the finish line.

Can you believe it?

Forty-four miles today would be one of the shorter days I would ride. Thirty miles away is Cambridge City, Indiana. Dave and I will meet there to swap batteries while Brian and Emmitt cruise ahead to Richmond to scout our spot for the night.

Because Google Maps is mostly sending me in every direction but the right one, I decide to take Route 40 straight into Richmond. Some locals told us this might be a mistake. There's usually heavy traffic on the very busy road, it being a major artery and all. I'm nervous leaving Knightstown, but Route 40 turns out to be a great choice. It's a two lane divided highway very much like Route 36, but traffic isn't that bad and I have a wide shoulder to ride on.

The weather is perfect again with very little wind and I arrive in Cambridge City at 9:30 a.m. I make such good time that I beat Dave there by half an hour. I call him and tell him I'm waiting at a church right off of Main Street (Route 40). The church has electrical outlets outside so it should work for our recharge. With all of our running around last night we only have one battery charged this morning.

Dave soon finds me but to our chagrin the outlets don't work. I sit in my chair in the shade of the church as Dave scouts for another place to charge the battery. He comes back five minutes later and says the local library looks promising.

"Where is it?" I ask pensively.

"Right over there." He points to a building about 50 yards away.

"Duh. OK, let's go."

It's 10 a.m. and we throw my chair into the van. I pedal three blocks to the library and again, to our chagrin, we find the library doesn't open until 1 p.m. Well, shit. I'm locking my bike to a bike rack outside the library magically hoping the sign was wrong and the door would fly open—actually I'm just exasperated and hoping for a miracle somewhere, somehow, when Dave points across Main Street and says, "What about there?"

He motions toward a dive bar. The door is propped open with a rock. A dive bar open at 10:30 a.m. when not even the library is open? What? I finish locking up my bike while Dave jogs across the street hoping for a Hail Mary. Of course I want the bar to be open, but we'd probably have to buy beer while we charged the battery (if they even let us) and it was damn early for that. But I'm always up for a beer, so what the hell. Dave disappears under the neon Pabst sign and I trot across the street shortly after.

I slowly open the door thinking I don't want to interrupt the cleaning people or a delivery kid restocking the beer coolers. It's dark and dingy and smells of stale beer and even staler cigarettes. The perfect dive. It takes a moment for my eyes to adjust. There's one patron at the bar. One patron. And an older gentleman behind the bar. I assume he must be the owner.

Dave is already sitting at a corner table with his laptop open, sucking off the Wi-Fi and doing our daily social media. He got the Wi-Fi but I know he hadn't asked about the battery. Wi-Fi was his thing, the battery was mine.

I explain my predicament to the barkeep. At first he's cautious, if not a little standoffish. But the patron at the counter, upon hearing my tale of riding from Denver to Indiana, turns and slaps a crisp $20 bill on the bar. "This is for your trip," he says with slurred lips. Remember, it was 10:30 in the a.m. But this guy is friendly and I like him right away. I figure he worked the night shift in town somewhere and was coming in for a pre-sleep night cap.

With the help of the barfly's good attitude, the owner slowly warms up to our situation and allows us to charge the battery at one of the booths. I order a burger and a beer, figuring we'll be here awhile. Besides, if I'm sucking this guy's electricity, it seems the least I can do. With the battery fully charged, I try to pay for lunch but the barkeep won't take my money. He even lets me bring my bike inside so I can keep an eye on it. We end up being there over three hours, and before we leave we take some pictures, me with a full cheeseburger belly, Dave being caught up with social media.

In the meantime, Brian and Emmitt have found a campground for the night just outside of Richmond, Indiana, on the Ohio side and are happily setting up camp. With me now on full battery, Dave charges ahead and waits at the Ohio state line to film me crossing with my arms raised high. I'm finally approaching my home state, our last and final state.

'We're going to finish!' I think excitedly. 'We are actually going to pull this shit off! Against all odds!'

It is a great feeling.

Dr. Robert Muckle, my specialist at Denver Ear Associates, worked hard to help me manage the Monster. He was my number ten doctor and took the time to dive into my two-inch-thick medical records.

As a neurotologist he knew plenty about MD. The past five years he's been the only doctor I've seen, and if I have anything to do with it, he will be the last.

Now I'm on a low-salt diet, less than 1500 mg per day. I also take a daily diuretic and keep diazepam on hand in case of emergencies. He did three procedures on my ear to help control my vertigo. Intratympanic gentamicin injections, as they're called—and it helped me immensely.

I almost had a halfway normal life when in the fall of 2019 I traveled to Kentucky to visit my mother and her husband Larry. I was only there for three weeks and was laid up on the couch the whole time. Larry sat next to me in his recliner, CPAP machine whirring away. I felt awful, and he felt worse. He was battling major heart issues and was doing kidney dialysis two times a week. We watched sports all day and old westerns all night. Neither of us slept well and I think he enjoyed my company. Larry became my hero those three weeks as I watched him fight for his life, and it made an impact on me in a big way.

Driving home to Colorado I thought a lot about how I fought daily for survival, and how

Larry did the same with grace and dignity. He passed away in the spring of 2020, but not before he planted in my mind the idea that I needed to do something big. Something special. That was the moment the idea of doing a cross-country trip grew like a seed in my heart. The bike trip I imagined would not necessarily be done solely in his honor, but it kind of was. He inspired me to represent myself and all who suffer like I do, and try to make a dent in the fucked-up world of chronic illness.

I thought that if I could keep my symptoms somewhat in check, maybe just maybe, I could make a difference. Maybe I could pull off the unimaginable. The impossible. According to the Adventure Cycling Association, 1,000 people do a Trans-American bike ride each summer. But I'm going to say this flat out: Not many do it as sick as me. Am I bragging? You're damn right I am.

Six months after Larry's death, I called Dave for the first time about the trip. I knew this would be a challenge of unproportioned meaning. Not only for me, but for all those who suffer chronic illness. I'm not a hero, but I decided I'd be one sick man trying to make a difference. We all miss you Larry. "Peace out" for eternity, my friend.

PART 7

Ohio: Home State Homecoming

Richmond, Indiana-Dayton, Ohio, 41 miles
Dayton, Ohio-London, Ohio, 49 miles
London, Ohio-Columbus, Ohio, 34 miles
Worthington, Ohio-Westerville, Ohio, 5.5 miles

CHAPTER 34

Once again Brian came through strong. He found a near empty campground outside Richmond, Indiana, on the Ohio side of the border. He had made friends with the host and got us a discount because of our trip. He gave the camp host a flyer explaining that Dave and I would be showing up in a couple hours. The host was very generous. Again, the generosity of middle America gave me hope for the future of our country.

I'm a cynical bastard at heart, and I fly no flag politically, but people everywhere were making this trip special. We were listened to, given free places to camp, had many meals donated or outright bought for us. People donated their hard-earned cash and prayed for us everywhere we went (especially in Kansas). As a country, there's a strong love for each other, rural or inner city, it doesn't matter. I hope we continue to do this for the sake of future generations. Ok, enough said on that.

Rolling toward Richmond, the weather is still holding and my forecast looks good. I'm four days away from ground zero (the end) and it's not lost on me in the least what we have accomplished thus far. We have flown by the seat of our pants for nearly a month and we are finally inside our last state. At least Brian and Emmitt are. Dave has hung at the Ohio border to Instagram my crossing as it happens, and I raise my hands high in simultaneous relief and disbelief that we've actually pulled it off.

At the campground I pitch the orange bubble behind Mallory and we sit around enjoying the small things that got us here. We play some games and call it a night. I slump into the orange bubble, turn on another ball game, and raise another middle finger to the Monster.

Tomorrow, Brian and Emmitt would be headed back to Columbus for Emmitt's driver's test. (He passed by the way.) Dave and I wouldn't see them again until my last day's ride into Columbus

Ohio has a great bike path system and I was looking forward to taking full advantage of it. Riding on the bike paths was always a good thing. The best thing. No traffic, no trucks, no car parts and broken glass in the shoulder to avoid. It was always a lot less stressful.

Halfway to Dayton the next day I get an instant message from a long-lost friend from 25 years ago. "Hey, it's Terry. Your last social media post said you were coming through London, Ohio."

"Yes I am," I reply, deep into enjoying a perfect day on the bike path.

"I live there now!" Terry says, excitedly. "You can stay at my place!"

How do these things keep happening? A free place to stay and another reunion with someone I love whom I haven't seen in forever?

Hot damn!

"Plan on it, buddy," I tell him. "Can't wait to see you." This is great news that cheers me greatly on an already awesome day.

Back before the trip started, I posted a near approximation of my route on social media and in my Ménière's support groups. I was fishing. Fishing for people like myself with Ménière's. As I said before, Dave and I wanted to meet and interview whoever would be available and willing, and post it on social media.

Enter Amanda Jew. Amanda emailed me personally and said, "I have Ménière's and I live in Dayton. I'll meet up with you if you want."

That was a month ago. I told her that would be great, the only issue was I wasn't sure when I'd be in Dayton, or if I'd be anywhere close to where she lived.

"Doesn't matter," she said. "Contact me when you know for sure and I'll see what I can do."

"Will do," I happily replied.

So last night in Richmond I had Dave get in touch with her to see if she was still interested. She said she was free tomorrow afternoon and would meet us wherever. This was great! I figured I'd book a hotel, the last one of our trip, so we'd have one last break and a good place to do the interview.

With more than a little agility, I traverse some crazy, busy streets to get through lower downtown Dayton. Turns out Google Bitch has again taken me on some crazy route that looked good on 'paper,' but was in fact nutty and nonsensical. Our hotel is in the eastern suburbs and despite Google Maps, I manage to get to the hotel safely and in time to meet Amanda.

This will be the third 'menierdo' I would have the pleasure to meet and I'm jacked! Well, as jacked as I could be, being exhausted from rolling across the country and having Ménière's.

Anywho, we check into a Hilton Tru around 2 p.m. Amanda would meet us around 4 p.m. depending on traffic. We make quick friends with the front desk clerk and she even lets me leave my bike in her office while Dave and I go out for a quick bite while our room is being prepared.

I picked the Hilton Tru for two reasons:

#1-It was on the northeast side of the city so I wouldn't have to navigate Dayton in the morning.

#2-Hilton Tru lobbies are very retro and atmospheric. The perfect place for an interview.

Our second story room overlooks the parking lot and I anxiously glance out the window every couple minutes. Eventually a red sedan pulls up right below our window. I watch closely.

"Is that her?" Dave asks.

"Give me a sec, I'll tell you when she gets out."

When Amanda steps out she does so very deliberately, slowly, and holding on to the car for support. Bingo. I've exited cars a thousand times and it was like looking in a mirror. "Yep," I say. "That's her."

Her husband Bobby was driving and I thought it was awesome that he came along. We haven't yet interviewed a spouse of someone with Ménière's and love the idea of that angle for the interview as well. But also, his wife was meeting two strange dudes at a hotel. You bet your ass he was coming.

We drop a floor on the elevator and cross the lobby, me running my hand along the wall for support. After introductions, it becomes comfortable real quick. Even with Ménière's, Amanda has a mad sense of humor. I love that the most. When people with chronic illness battle to survive each day and can still manage a sense of humor, that's priceless. Also, she's cute as a button and a full-on crack-up, not to mention her husband Bobby is cool as shit. He's about my height, but built solid. Dark complexioned and reserved, he was quiet and observant. Though gentle in spirit, I knew he could kick my ass three ways to Tuesday if need be. But the guy was a teddy bear. He and Amanda make a great couple and are both honest and candid about their lives and struggles with the Monster.

When filming is over we ask Amanda if she wants to go outside and help us do the end-of-day video.

Enthusiastic "Yes!"

It was getting to the point where people watching us from across America felt excited to insert themselves into the story they'd been watching. We loved that and felt honored. By now, nearly everyone knew our signature, "Peace Out!" and wouldn't miss their opportunity to be the one to chime in. We make one of our favorite and most silly videos with Amanda, which involves swapping a beer for the now infamous Hall and Oates shirt.

It's a great visit and as we part ways, I think what an honor it is to have another kindred spirit in the battle.

The best to you and Bobby, Amanda. You are the greatest. Peace out, Girl!

CHAPTER 35

Ping: "Take a left on Elizabeth Street." You've got to be fucking kidding me.

I left the Hilton Tru an hour ago and the morning is cool and crisp. I feel better than I have in days after a good night sleep and a needed shower. Google Lady has gotten me to the park where I would switch to another bike path. But like I said before, this was an up and down relationship. And hearing the ping and the absurd directions to once again find a non-existent Elizabeth Street makes me want to rip her head off.

I'm riding in circles around a big suburban park on the northeast side of Dayton. But when I enter the park I discover multiple paths leading in and out. Strips of smooth black asphalt intersect from every direction. I have no idea which one goes to London, Ohio, our goal for today.

I plead with Google Bitch (who I now rename Elizabeth) to help me navigate this unfamiliar park. I stop pedaling and come to a slow crawl holding my breath as I hope she can get her shit straight.

Ping! "Take a left on Elizabeth Street," Google Bitch says again.

You suck Google Maps! I go into a tirade and give her an earful. Then I turn her off. 'I don't need this shit right now,' I fume.

I slam my brakes and screech to a stop. I actually put my foot down this time, though. This can't be as hard as I'm making it. The trees in the park are thick and add to my disorientation. I park my bike and sit on a bench. I need to talk myself off the ledge. 'I've only been riding for an hour and I have all day,' I think as I try to calm myself.

Dave and I researched my route last night where I

would navigate four trails. The first to the park, then I needed to find Creekside Trail, but it's a chaotic mess. The Creekside Trail would take me through the town of Xenia, Ohio, where I would transfer to the Prairie Grass Trail. After that I would get on The Ohio to Erie Trail. Sounds simple, I know, but it's me we're talking about here. So I shut Google Bitch down and decide to wing it.

I look over and see two moms pushing heavy duty jogging strollers toward my bench. "Excuse me, but can you ladies tell me where I pick up the Creekside Trail heading east?"

One of the toddlers sits quietly holding a dump truck on his lap. He glares at me from his $2,000 seat on wheels, wondering what the holdup is. Then he sees my bike and becomes instantly mesmerised by the large, pink machine covered in shiny stickers. He points wildly, losing all interest in his truck. I get off my bench and push my bike over in front of him so he can get a better look. He lights up like a Christmas tree on full tilt.

One of the super moms points in the direction they had just come. "It goes through that end of the park."

I thank them and pedal away in that direction. I glance down at the toddler one last time. 'This is my toy kid, get your own.' Unfortunately, I still have to ask directions one more time to find the right trail. But it's better than the stress of navigating the park with Elizabeth telling me to find streets that don't exist.

Creekside Trail is dynamite. It meanders along a river, tree-lined with overhanging shade and I'm super comfortable on it. I'll be on bike paths all the way to Columbus now and it feels great knowing traffic and trucks are a thing of the past. The one downfall is that these trails, in or near a city, are heavily utilized. You got Lance Armstrong wannabes buzzing me from all directions, down to your family of five taking up the whole path with stupid-wide training wheels. Only on straightaways where I see no other people do I even attempt to open it up. Twenty-five to 30 miles per hour doesn't sound fast, but when everyone else is doing ten miles an hour at best, it can seem Dale Earnhardt, Jr. is screaming through. I try to be courteous and more than a little cautious. An errant swerve into a toddler would be disastrous.

And that's when it happened.

I round a random bend, the river on my right with thick trees on my left. It's a fantastic, very long and empty straight away. I click my gears up to turbo. It's time to have some fun.

Well . . . it wasn't fun for the squirrel.

I glance down at my speedometer and see 28 miles per hour. When I glance back up, I see him. Fifty feet ahead on the left a squirrel sits with a pine cone or some shit in its hands. I immediately know exactly how this is going to go. I just know in my gut.

I actually say out loud, "Don't do it, buddy! Don't do it!"

But, of course, in normal squirrel fashion, at the last second he makes a break for it. Straight across my path. Goddamn it. My front tire hits him square in his furry little midsection. Crunch! Game over.

Now, I've seen my share of roadkill on this trip—skunks, snakes, opossums, deers, coyotes, and anything else stupid enough to walk into highway traffic. But never on a bike path. I wonder what the next biker will think about the squirrel splattered in two. My guess is, 'What would be going so fast to cause this?' The answer is simple: Me, on a fucking E-bike.

I cruise through Xenia without slicing any more wildlife in half and meet a guy named 'Dave' who's out for a pleasant morning ride. We catch the Ohio to Erie

Trail together and enjoy a casual chat for the last 20 miles. Brother Dave is in the van up ahead in Cedarville. He parks at the town library and rides back to meet me on his bike. The two Daves and I cruise along chatting, and today would be one of my favorite rides of the trip. The weather is perfect, the company exceptional, and all was well in the world. Except for the squirrel who wouldn't be coming home for dinner. But that aside . . .

I arrive at Terry's house mid-afternoon. Terry is taller than I, but if you can believe it, he's skinnier. Except for our beer bellies. Those are pretty much identical, like golf balls stuck in a straw. Terry and I became friends in the early 90s and are like brothers. He has my kind of sense of humor spot-on and we would do anything for each other. Even after all these years—and it has been years—so we spent the evening catching up. I set up my tent in his backyard and Dave parks the van in the side yard.

This would be my last night in the orange bubble. I say this with a little sadness because I never had a bad night in the tent (props to North Face).

Of course Terry jumps in without hesitation when it comes to helping us make stupid videos. He's a total ham and our videos are hilarious.

Brian and my nephew Nathan would be driving the 33 miles to Terry's in the morning. Nathan has a film degree from The Ohio State University and would document our ride through networks of bike paths with a GoPro on his head and a drone in the air.

Dave, Brian and I would make the ride into Columbus together on bikes. Dave would come back to Terry's for the van once our trek to Brian's house was finished. Having both my brothers for the entire last leg was a gift. This was going to be my favorite day of riding, hands down. The thought of being upright and able to ride at this point in the trip was miraculous. Being able to enjoy it was pure ecstasy.

The next morning we take it slow and easy and truly enjoy each other's company and the amazing fall weather, which we'd enjoyed for days. But before leaving London, Terry dons a dress and a bright red wig and we do the morning video from a train museum next to his house. He acts like my forlorn lover who was sad I was leaving for Columbus and I hop on my bike at the end and yell, "I did it!" with arms raised.

I had truly done it.

CHAPTER 36

The ride to Columbus is a blast. My brothers and I stop often to relax and relish the last leg. We take some more funny videos along the way (which we can't mention here for legal reasons).

The bike paths in Ohio, for the most part, are old train tracks ripped up and replaced with blacktop. Very straight and very scenic, and some still parallel active tracks. At one point we chuck my bike into an empty boxcar and Dave films me riding past the open door. He also films me running on top of a row of parked train cars. In the midst of our laughing and reverie, it's never far from my mind that at the end of today's ride I will be standing in Columbus, Ohio: Mission Accomplished.

We ride through south Columbus, past downtown, and up through The Ohio State University campus. We take some pics at the famous Horseshoe Stadium to send to my friend Ed in Colorado (OSU law grad and now a county judge) and eat some lunch.

Following the Olentangy River bike path north toward Brian's house in the suburb of Worthington, Dave whips past a random cyclist on the path. When he turns to see that Brian and I have stopped, he comes back and recognizes the stranger: Our Dad.

"Damn, I didn't even see you there," Dave says, befuddled.

It's understandable after the focus we'd been maintaining for what . . . 1400 plus miles across America? . . . he can be forgiven for that.

So we pick up my father and he rides the final five miles with us.

As you can imagine, arriving at Brian's house was beyond joyous for me. The weight of it all finally fell away. The weight of meeting expectations for the people who generously donated and sponsored my hair brained idea. The weight of everyone around the world who gave towards research on GoFundMe. We set the ridiculous goal of raising $10,000. We ended the trip with $10,040 donated.

Never in our wildest imaginations did we think that would happen. But it did. Three months ago "On the VertiGO" was an unrealized dream. And a million things could've gone wrong. But they didn't. In actuality, a million things went right. And arriving at my brother's house was my dream realized. I'm not saying it was easy, not by a long shot. Dave and I along with Bill, Bryce, Brian, and Emmitt earned every mile with blood, sweat and tears.

I pull into Brian's driveway to signs held by my sister-in-law, Susie, and a congratulatory jump into my body (not needed) by Rigbee, my brother's dog. After hugs all around, I go into the backyard and collapse in a chair. Time for decompression. Everyone had left, scrambling to retrieve vehicles. The van was still in London, my father's car was at the park where we met him five miles away.

I'm completely alone again and it feels great. I sit in the backyard in the shade, wondering if I made a difference. I thought I had, no matter how small it might have been. My bike is parked next to me in the backyard. I glance over at it. This has been my trusty steed, my iron horse for an entire month. I pushed it to its limits and more. And she held up. Resting my head back to keep it still, I sigh, and enjoy the shade.

I spend the next hour reminiscing. My thoughts return to the uncertain and anxious days before we left. I revisit the heat of Kansas, the cold rain in Missouri, the God sent people of Illinois. I inwardly smile reminding myself of the beautiful weather in Indiana and Ohio, perfect days riding bikes with my family. But all that pales in comparison to the weight of the Monster who rode shotgun with me each and every mile. Other than the people I met, my battle with MD is what I'll remember the most. I have no choice. I'll go back to my couch and it will go with me. The war will rage on long after my trip becomes a faint memory.

I hope my journey inspired some people, but that's not the point. I've inspired myself. So in this moment of reflection, I'm grateful, thankful and at peace . . . in the shade.

In my life I'm surrounded by people who love me, and during one desperate month in September, I learned to love myself.

CHAPTER 37

My trip was complete, yet I still had one more job to do—meet the mayor. Five and a half miles tomorrow from Worthington to Westerville, a drop in the bucket. It'd be another beautiful weather day and another ride with my two brothers, our Dad, and my nephew Nathan. The finish line would be town hall in the suburb where I grew up.

Last week Mayor Cocuzzi and I had discussed a noon arrival, so the team and I spread the word that we'd meet at a local park near Brian's house if anyone wanted to ride. This would also provide a nice gathering spot for friends and family who wanted to just come by and wish me well, those who'd followed me cross-country on social media.

We arrive at the park and it doesn't disappoint. Friends are there in spades, many I haven't seen in years because I'd been living in Colorado since 1998.

My mother drove up from Kentucky. My dad drove in once again to ride his bike with me to Westerville. My friends Atticus and Chuck come by, and longtime friend Chris H. even brings the town manager of Worthington for a meet and greet. Of course we couldn't pass up the opportunity to put a local official in one of our videos, so the town manager and I do the morning send-off video with friends and family spread in the background. I loved it. And I felt like crap.

It was a tough day. I was exhausted and nervous about meeting the mayor, and all that on top of normal Ménière's symptoms. I wish I could say I enjoyed the day as much as the previous few awesome days on Ohio's bike paths. But I can't. I was Miserable with a capital 'M,' but those who knew me best gave a lot of grace and latitude to carry me through the day.

Exhaustion is another curse of MD. It's always present in some form or other. Physical exhaustion is hard, but emotional exhaustion is worse. And I was at the worse end of the curve. I had tested myself like never before and I was flat wiped out. I could barely stand up, much less lead a triumphant charge down State Street. I was proud of our accomplishment, but was having a tough time taking it in. I felt like shit. This was a bad day, and I knew it the second I rolled out of bed.

That being said, our small gang of bikers push off from the park at 11:15 a.m. for our noon meeting with the mayor. On the way, we ride past the barbershop where my father gets his haircut. My dad told me he was there a few weeks ago when his barber mentioned something he'd seen in the local paper: "Apparently some guy who grew up here is going to ride his bike from Denver to Westerville and he's got some weird disease. Did you see that?"

My dad laughed, "Yeah, that's my son."

As we glide past the shop, my dad asks if we could stop in and say "Hi." The guys would love to meet me.

"Of course."

The guys at the barbershop seem a bit starstruck and that buoys my spirits a bit on a day I wish I hadn't gotten out of bed. But their enthusiasm is contagious and they even donate a check right then and there for $100. Wow, worth the stop indeed. The whole crew at the shop is great, and we stand out front talking for a bit.

After some chit and chat, we're right on schedule for our noon arrival at town hall. Our troop deftly navigates the streets of uptown Westerville until we arrive to family and friends packed along the sidewalk with signs, balloons, shouts of goodwill, and even a few cowbells if I remember correctly. A local reporter takes photos for a follow-up article that would appear in the next week's local newspaper.

Mayor Cocuzzi welcomes me and is very hospitable. She asks me questions about my trip and we chat amicably for a few minutes as I try my best to appear lucid and not wobbly.

I feel terrible, but don't want to ruin the day. All I could do was picture my couch back in Colorado and how much I wished I was there instead of meeting the mayor. You see, that's what Ménière's does. It robs you of a normal life. You never know when the Monster will strike and if it strikes the one time in your life when you're meeting the mayor of your hometown, then that's what you get, and there's not a goddamn thing you can do about it.

People around those who suffer from Ménière's really need to be aware of this. It's not that we don't want to do things or are making excuses to get out of things. Far from it. Our lives are robbed of the predictability most others take for granted. Scheduling a trip to the grocery can be a tremendous trauma for us in a way no healthy person can understand.

That's why I appreciated meeting John and Sue and Amanda as I wove my way across America. They get it. And Bobby gets it, living with Amanda. It's not pretty. It's just not. There's no way to dress it up and certainly no way to explain everything I've said in this book about Ménière's to the mayor of Westerville standing right in front of me. She'd never know how I felt or what I was going through. I just hope she wasn't too put off by the fact that all my energy was going into just standing up, much less trying to be charming and upbeat for our conversation.

But after preliminary niceties, she presents me with a check from the city for $100 to put towards research. Then she hands me a goody bag to go with it. I'm floored by her and the city's generosity and am truly appreciative and honored. I graduated from Westerville South High School back in 1985 where most of the kids didn't even know my name. And here I am now, The Prodigal Son of Westerville returned home and acknowledged by the mayor. The only thing that would've made it more sweet is if I didn't feel like crap the whole time. But you know, that's why I'm here meeting the mayor in the first place. To get the word out. To help those with this torturous condition feel less lonely and a little more empowered.

Throughout the trip we'd get comments all the time from Ménière's warriors who'd report that we inspired them to get off the couch and ride their bike, or go for a run, or take a walk around the block—an activity some of them hadn't done in *years*. And I had the privilege to lead that charge against the Monster.

Once again, up yours Ménière's! You can't—you won't—keep us down!

After wrapping up at town hall, we invite any and all who want to join, to meet in a town park down the road. We're going to throw a pizza party! Those on bikes ride the few blocks and everyone else just kind of shows up. It's festive and relaxing, and again, the weather is beyond fantastic. I spend the entire time in my camp chair.

My dad had worn the Hall and Oates shirt the whole way for our morning ride. Now we throw it on my mom for a quick photo op, holding a slice of cheese pizza in her hand. Not sure she really knew who it was or the significance of it, but we do it anyway and she's a great sport.

Now I was officially done. And I couldn't be more proud. We're taking turns at the park restroom before leaving and that's when I feel it.

Oh, no. Not now, not here. This is bullshit. I feel another vertigo attack coming on.

Unlike the day in Taylorville when I didn't carry my meds with me, today I have them in my bike rack bag. I learned my lesson the incredibly hard way to never be anywhere without them again. So with shaky hands and sweat dripping from my forehead, I unzip my bag and down a 2 mg tablet of Diazepam. I slump against the wall of the restroom, lay my head back on the cool brick, and tell the guys I need a minute.

Luckily that day I managed to stave off a bad attack, but I couldn't help telling the Monster one last time, 'You bastard. On the VertiGO is now done and over. So screw you. But being the Monster you are, it makes sense that you'd try to get the last word, try to get one final blow. But fuck you. One last time for the trip, Fuck. You.'

I climb on my bike still feeling like shit. I exit the park managing to raise my middle finger one last time in salute. I beat you. You got your blows in, but at the end of the day, I won. I beat you. You couldn't keep me down, and now the world knows it.

Up yours, Ménière's Disease. You lost.

Meniere's: On the Vertigo · 🔔
Sep 25, 2020 · 🌐

Meeting the Mayor of Westerville!!

Living with Ménière's disease or anything that makes daily survival a challenge is not fair. But no one's promised a fair life. My chronic illness is something I deal with every second of every day. Getting off my couch or out of bed twice a day to walk my dog is my life now. It's every day, it's every week, and it's turning into every year.

Is this all I get?

If so, I need to dig deeper. And I mean dig deeper than I've ever dug before. I want answers.

A good friend of mine and spiritual mentor Nancy Black told me years ago, "Something will come of this. I don't know what yet and I can't tell you how it will play out," but she did look me straight in the eyes and said, "But it will be something you don't expect and it will be truly great. Beyond what you can imagine."

At that moment she wasn't blowing smoke up my ass. She wasn't making any promises. But she believed in me and my resilience. At the time I didn't feel resilient. I thought her words were foolishness, fodder only fit for a fire. But she witnessed one of my worst vertigo attacks ever, so she wasn't that stupid. She knew the life I lived. But again, to me, all those years ago, those were empty words falling on my ringing ears. Nothing good was going to come of this. How could it? There's no cure. No one even knows what causes it. Truly, what the bloody hell is going on here? My life is literally in the ashcan of human experience and enjoyment. It's 24/7 torture, and that's no exaggeration.

So wanting to do a bike trip was something I'd kept secret for over six months. If I ever went public with it, I would surely end up the fool. And the second Dave and I went public, the weight of it was overwhelming, I can't even describe it.

A week after Dave agreed to be my ride support, I was golfing with my good friend Kevin Shafer and his parents Jack and Marcia. It was Jack's birthday so I felt honored to be invited along. Golf is one thing Ménière's hasn't robbed me of, though trying to hit a good shot while feeling like you're on the deck of the Titanic can be quite the challenge. Anyway, halfway through the round, well actually on the 14th tee, I mentioned in passing that I might do a bike trip to raise money and awareness for my disease, with which they were all very familiar. All three stopped cold in their tracks. Right there on the 14th tee box they wanted to hear more.

I explained my vision and my mind blew sideways for a minute.

Would they flinch?

Or would they merely give me an overly compassionate pat on the back, like I was a puppy or something, saying, 'Hey, we love you but that sounds insane...'

But to my surprise, all three sets of eyes lit up with the possibility of seeing me do something great. And that moment changed everything. They did not hesitate or question my sanity. They believed. And in that moment, with the baby finally out in the world, I finally believed.

They said they would donate: Whatever it took, whatever you need. I will be eternally grateful for their enthusiasm and support on a day when it could have all died in one punch. If they had reacted differently, there's no way I would've gone forward. No way.

I wanted to understand my lot in life, and I wasn't going to figure it out lying on my couch year after year. I knew I'd be pushing myself, and others, beyond my and their comfort zones. Even more so I'd be pushing the disease riddling my body to a breaking point. I needed to push back on this disease as hard as it was pushing on me. One month, my rules.

After Dave and I went public with the trip, I was amazed at the support from family and friends. Donations started rolling in from local businesses and friends and family, some of whom I hadn't talked to or seen for *years*, all of whom went above and beyond anything I could've imagined to make my trip a reality. But now, Dave and I thought, with the word out and money rolling in, we had to actually pull this off. And we did. We did!

A few weeks after returning home to Colorado, I sat down to write out my thoughts. What did I learn? Or did I learn anything at all? How does living with a chronic illness fit in my life and those around me? And this is what came out:

Everyone is living a story. And I thought Ménière's Disease had completely pulled me out of MY story. For eight years I grieved the loss of my old self. My story was interrupted; not only that, my story came to a screeching halt. Now I realize that MD was a *part* of my story. Not a burden to carry, or something that's ended my life, but it's who I am, and it always was!

My previous life was training me, preparing me, so that I could carry this life-changing disease with grace, dignity, and hopefully more than a little agility.

I still fear vertigo attacks and bad days, but I no longer fear my part in it. This is what debilitates a person with a chronic illness—Fear. The fear that I'm not now who I was meant to be. But I realized this WAS who I was meant to be.

It doesn't mean I now love the Monster, but it means I don't have to be afraid of who I am becoming. I'm still worthy of love, and respect, and living my life

to the fullest, no matter what that looks like to the outside world. This is my story. And it always was. It's everyone's story. The good, the bad and the ugly.

And believe it or not, even though I swore the whole trip I would go back to my couch and give the bike I would never ride again to my wife, I actually got up and rode the next day. And the next. Until it finally snowed and I could ride no more.

So for now, I'm going to keep pushing forward and do my best to live with grace and dignity.

Wishing you all more good days than bad days.
Till the next ride, peace out!

FOLLOW US ON SOCIAL MEDIA:

 Instagram
@onthevertigo

 Facebook
Menieres: On the Vertigo

 Youtube
Dave Schwier – Meniere's On the VertiGO!

thank you

Dave and I would like to thank John Ingram with Deaf to Meniere's, and Joan Wincentsen with The American Hearing Research Foundation for graciously accepting the funds raised from this project. We know you will use the money wisely for research.

We also want to thank any and all who made this trip possible, in no particular order: Lucy with Wilderness Sports, Dillon, CO. Chris with Locals Liquors, Silverthorne, CO. Kevin Shafer with Shafer Photography, Aurora, CO. Jack and Marcia Shafer with Shafer Woodworking, CA. Cory with Bakers Brewery, Silverthorne, CO. Reser Bicycle Outfitters, Newport, KY. Columbine Country Club, Littleton, CO. Martha Brown with Advantage Brokerage Group, Loveland, CO. Cam and Rita with A-1 Auto, Breckenridge, CO. Dr Robert Muckle with Denver Ear Associates, Denver, CO. Dave and Becca Lawless with Big Walnut Golf Course, Sunbury, OH.

Friends and family who went above and beyond, in no particular order: Emily Schwier, Nolan Schwier, Julie Duncan, Stephanie Houston, Karen and Garth Walker, Jim and Carol Schwier, Jeremy (Moe) Esch, Brian Clifford, Ed and Allison Casias, Jeremy and Nancy Black, Aaron Steck, Susan Carson, Bill Dyke, Warren and LaRea Dyke, Brian, Susie, Ayla and Emmitt Schwier, Mark Petrovich, Bryce and Isabel Lawson, Nathan and Heather Sergio, Jennica Sergio, Brad Jacobson, Gina Manchego Zufall, Scott and Andrea Anderson, Chuck Keene, Atticus Myser, Chris Hasebrook, Warren Leagas, Janet Doolan, Bess Raines, Adrienne Smith, Nichole Counts, Terry Rennecker and Kimberly Rinehart. Jim and Mary Lynn Coratti, Sue Endsley, Bobby and Amanda Jew, Harry Sparrow, Carmen Ensinger with *Scott County Times*, Marla K. Kuhlman and Shane Flanigan with *This Week Westerville News*, Mayor Kathy Cocuzzi, Antonio Olivero with *Summit Daily News*. And all my peeps at MWW, you know who you are.

Thanks to the editors of this manuscript for their painstaking attention to detail. In no particular order: Garth Walker, Kathy Bohnam, and Pamela Sibert-Hooker.

Special thank you to Pamela Sibert-Hooker for her time and technical expertise in layout, formatting and interior design of the book. You are the best, Pam. A simple 'thank you' falls far short of our actual appreciation for everything you do.

We'd also like to thank Nathan Sergio, a magician of technology and design, for consulting, donating and training Dave on all things technical for our trip, and for producing our cover. Even with a baby on the way, he still made time for us.

Thanks to Brian Schwier for branding our trip 'On the VertiGO!' (Death Race 2020 wouldn't cut it, and that's all I was coming up with when Brian's creativity saved the day.) Well done, and now we're even for me stranding you on the bike path in Coatsville.

Many thanks also go to those on Facebook and Instagram who followed every challenge and triumph of the trip as it was happening in real time. We were encouraged, buoyed and energized by your constant comments and support.

Last but not least (in the least), we want to thank Robin R. Lyons of Winchester, Ill, for everything he did for us, the scope of which reached far beyond his small town. Never have we met a person so instantly gracious, welcoming and giving to a rag-tag group of complete strangers who randomly showed up on his doorstep one sunny Sunday afternoon. We are eternally grateful and will remember you forever, my friend.

ON THE VERTIGO

Ménière's Disease Awareness

E-Bike Trip Across America

Photo Album

~ Somewhere between Colorado and Ohio ~

~September of 2020 ~

~ Planet Earth ~

welcome
316

Meniere's: On the Vertigo · 🔔
Sep 12, 2020 · 🌐

Thank you, Bill! You're the best and we will miss you as we travel on.

Meniere's: On the Vertigo • 🔔
Sep 16, 2020 • 🌐

Morning send-off featuring Brian Schwier!

Meniere's: On the Vertigo · 🔔
Sep 21, 2020 · 🌐

Evening wrap-up day 21—We're in Ohio!

Meniere's: On the Vertigo · 🔔
Sep 22, 2020 · 🌐

Fellow Meniere's warrior Amanda does the
end of day wrap-up from Dayton, OH!

PEACE OUT!

Made in the USA
Middletown, DE
14 April 2021